Penguin Education
BIOLOGY TOPIC BOOKS
General editor: Margaret Sands

Human populations

David Hay

'This is nothing, you should be here
in the rush hour.'

David Hay

Human populations

Penguin Books

Penguin Books Ltd, Harmondsworth, Middlesex, England
Penguin Books Inc, 7110 Ambassador Road, Baltimore, Md 21207, USA
Penguin Books Australia Ltd, Ringwood, Victoria, Australia

First published 1972
Copyright © David Hay, 1972

Designed by Arthur Lockwood

Photoset in Malta by St Paul's Press Ltd.
Made and printed in Great Britain by Compton Printing Ltd, London and Aylesbury
Set in Lumitype Times Roman

Introduction   page 7

1 **Human population growth**   8

2 **Fertility**   18

3 **Mortality**   26

4 **Migrations**   36

5 **Traditional peoples**   48

6 **Modern population growth**   56

7 **Population control**   70

8 **Industrial populations**   82

Further information   90

Index   94

Acknowledgements   96

Introduction

Many alarming and conflicting things are said about the world's population and the population explosion. How can we tell what to believe?

In this book I have tried to look at this problem in the light of general population biology. Man is not really an outside observer of a vast collection of plants, animals, rocks and so on. We are, in fact, inseparable from the rest of nature and must respect the needs of the whole living community in order to survive.

The increasing size of the human population is the most obvious pressure on the Earth's resources. There are many things that can be learnt from studies of animal populations which will help us to understand human populations. However, this is an area of considerable controversy, and there are a number of difficulties in making strict comparisons between animals and human beings. For example, do studies on overcrowding in rat populations really shed light on similar human situations? The biological effects of being crowded together *might* be the same in rats and men, but this could well be hidden in man by his complicated traditions of how people are supposed to behave in a crush. Clearly, we do not know many answers, and arguments often hinge around extremely subtle points, so I have avoided going into much detail on controversial subjects. I hope the book will entertain and stimulate its readers to find out more about a part of biology with a practical importance for all our futures.

Apart from my debt to many writers on subjects relating to population, I would like to mention Peter Davies, Margaret Sands, John Peberdy (all of Nottingham University), Michael Buttler of Penguin Education and my wife, Jane. All of these either gave advice, read the book or did both.

Overpopulation, as
visualized in an
engraving by George
Cruikshank in 1851.

1 Human population growth

At present rates of growth, in nine hundred years time the human population will be so dense that the entire land and sea will have to be covered by a continuous two-thousand-storey building to house and 'service' everybody. That is the prediction of J. H. Fremlin, a British physicist. This will be the absolute limit to the population the earth can carry. Whether we could bear to live practically imprisoned in our seven and a half square metres of floor space, having food and air piped in and wastes piped out, is another matter. This population explosion is very worrying and it is important to know more about the ways populations grow.

Animal populations

If you ask a biologist about population, he will talk about increasing numbers of bacteria or yeast cells growing in a test-tube of liquid food. Or he may talk about an aquarium gradually filling with water fleas, or perhaps of species of beetle living in a jar of flour, competing for food and space. His definition of population is: *the number of organisms of the same species occupying a particular space.*

Experiment to count yeast cells

In this experiment, a biologist would place a small number of yeast cells in a test-tube containing sterile dilute syrup. Every half-hour he draws off a small sample with a pipette and examines it under a microscope. One simple way of following the development of the population is by counting the number of yeast cells in a standard area of the microscope slide. Each time he takes a sample, he can estimate the growth-rate of the whole population in the test tube. The graph illustrates the results of an experiment of this type, where the numbers of cells have been estimated over a period of twenty hours. You can see that at fifteen hours there are nearly 665 times as many cells as there were at the start of the experiment. Another point to notice is that the graph is S-shaped or *sigmoid*, and this shows that after a slow start, here lasting four hours, the population has built up very quickly. After twelve hours it began to slow down, and more or less stopped growing after fifteen hours. The population stays at this *optimum* level and does not keep on growing for ever, either because it has used up most of the food or because poisonous excretory substances from the yeast build up. The rate of reproduction cannot therefore be maintained. At this point, a balance is reached between the numbers reproduced and the numbers dying, corresponding to the maximum height shown on the graph. Many natural populations have this type of *growth curve*. If the solution containing the yeast cells is not changed, the lack of food or the poisonous substances will cause more and more cells to die until the whole colony is dead.

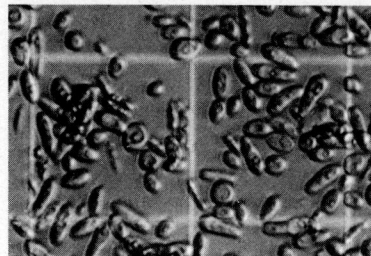

A magnified view of yeast on a counting slide. The slide is ruled into squares so that the number of yeast cells can be estimated. The S-shaped curve (below) could be built up from observations made in this way.

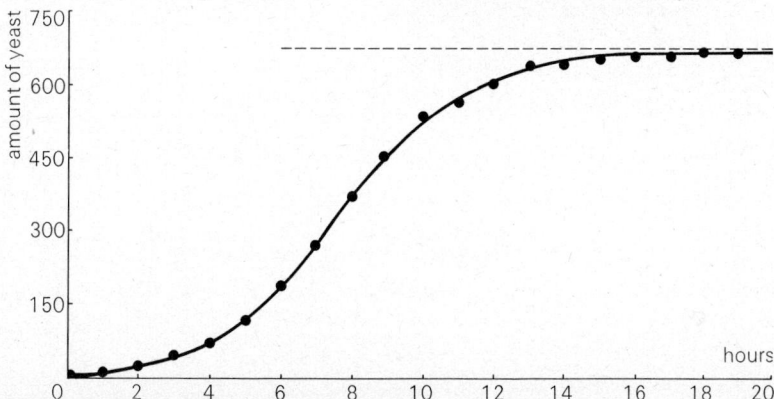

Biologists who study populations know more about what happens in populations of this kind than they do about larger animals and plants because small organisms are much more easily studied and cared for. Their lives are short enough to allow many generations of offspring to be produced in a few days or months, their food is usually something simple like flour or sugar, and the cost of keeping them in uniform conditions is very low. They are also easier to count than, say, human populations.

Studies of animals or small organisms in a laboratory give us a useful guide to what may be happening in the normal environment, but until measurements are made 'in the field' we cannot be sure that the two situations are similar. For many animals it is not possible to use laboratory techniques, and in this case we have to depend on field work alone. A classic example of this approach is D. A. MacLulich's account, published in 1937, of population changes in the snowshoe hare.

The snowshoe hare

The snowshoe hare lives in the Hudson Bay area of Canada, and records have been kept by the Hudson Bay Company of the number of skins taken by fur trappers since about 1800. Because he was unsure how accurate an estimate of the population was given by these figures, MacLulich also collected figures from the following sources:

1. Statements about numbers taken from old books and magazines.

2. Questionnaires to trappers about hare abundance.

3. Field work
   (i) trapping hares at chosen spots at regular intervals;
   (ii) censuses of various sorts;
   (iii) personal observations of hares;
   (iv) information derived from droppings seen.

MacLulich's estimate of population trends is from 1845 to 1935. If his figures are correct, it is obvious that population growth in the snowshoe hare does not stay at a maximum for any length of time. Instead, there is a series of violent fluctuations in numbers, each cycle taking approximately ten years.

The peaks of abundance are followed by *crashes*, when the hares become very scarce for one or two years.

These fluctuations are similar to the population pattern in a species of lynx which feeds on the hare. In the past the peak of abundance of the hares has always preceded that of the lynx by a year or so, and it has been suggested that, after the hares reach a maximum,

they become drastically reduced by disease or are eaten by the lynx, which is then reduced due to lack of prey. This seems reasonable enough, but to test the hypothesis you would have to show that the drop in hare numbers really was due to the fact that the lynx were eating them, and not to some other reason such as the shortage of food, or overcrowding.

A comparison of populations of the Canadian lynx and the snowshoe hare. Population 'crashes' in the hare are usually followed by a similar reduction in the number of lynx.

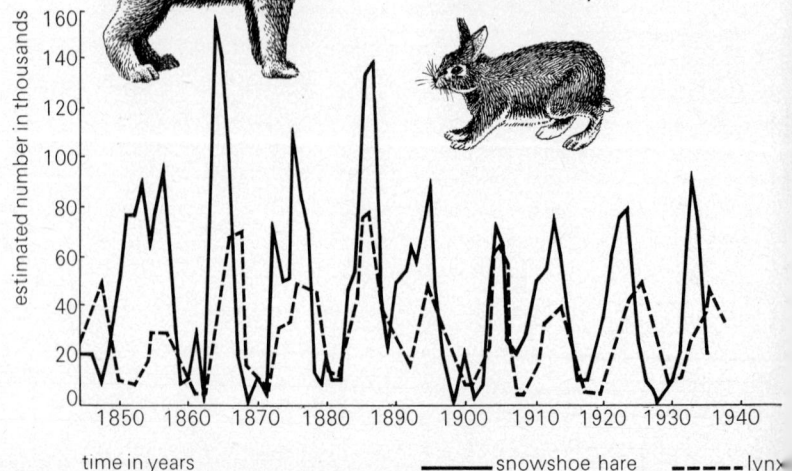

snowshoe hare ——— lynx - - - - -

Human populations

The growth curves for a laboratory population of yeast and for the snowshoe hare are opposite extremes. What happens in human populations? It is difficult to give a clear-cut answer because, compared with yeast or hares, man reproduces very slowly, so that long-term changes in population size must be measured in centuries or longer.

Usually there are no written records, and numbers have to be estimated. The practice of counting people at regular intervals is comparatively recent and is not universal, even today. The first official census in the United States was in 1790 and the first reliable census in England was not until 1841. Previously, occasional records of population counts were taken in various parts of the world. The most famous of these, the English Domesday census, was completed in 1086. Apart from sources of this kind, population estimates before the seventeenth century are little more than informed guesses and are the cause of considerable argument. Also, the further back you go in time, the fewer written records there are and the more you depend on speculation.

William de Percy holds Hambledon. He came by it along with his wife. Alwin held it from King Edward. It was then taxed as 8 hides. There is land for 3 ploughs. There is 1 plough on the demesne. Also there are 6 villeins and 6 bordars (cottagers) with 2 ploughs. There are 2 serfs and a mill worth 12 pence. There is a woodland worth 4 swine. In Edward's reign it was worth 4 pounds as it is now. When it first came to its present lord it was worth 3 pounds.

An extract from the Domesday book, with a translation. The Domesday survey, completed in 1086, is not a very reliable count of the population because it was made to help tax estimates and so many people evaded it. Allowing for this it is estimated that the population of England at this time was about 1·8–2 million.

Queen Victoria heads the entry for the Royal Household in the census of 1841.

An extract from the American Census of 1790.

NEW-HAMPSHIRE.

GRAFTON COUNTY.	Free white males of 16 years and upwards, including heads of families.	Free white males under 16 years.	Free white females, including heads of families.	All other free persons.	Slaves.	Total.
Haverhill, - - - -	163	118	266	1	4	552
Plymouth, - - - -	182	142	297		4	625
Alexandria, - - -	79	87	132			298
Bartlett, - - - -	55	57	135	1		248
Bath, - - - -	117	136	239	1		493
Bridgewater, - - -	84	62	134	1		281
Burton, - - - -	34	45	62			141
Cambridge, not inhabited						
Campton, - - - -	113	79	202	1		395
Canaan, - - - -	137	123	223			483
Chatham, - - - -	17	13	28			58
Cockburne, - - -	9	5	12			26
Cockermouth, - - -	94	104	175			373
Colburne, - - - -	10	6	13			29
Concord, alias Gunthwaite	91	75	147			313
Coventry, - - - -	21	20	47			88
Dalton, - - - -	3	4	7			14
Dartmouth, - - -	34	25	52			111

UK Census questions

1811

The overseer of each area had to provide answers to the following seven questions:

1. How many Inhabited Houses are there in your Parish, Township, or Place; and by how many Families are they occupied?
2. How many Houses are now building, and therefore not yet inhabited?
3. How many other Houses are uninhabited?
4. What Number of Families in your Parish, Township, or Place, are chiefly employed in and maintained by Agriculture; how many Families are chiefly employed in and maintained by Trade, Manufactures, or Handicraft; and how many Families are not comprized in either of the two preceding Classes?
5. How many Persons (including Children of whatever Age) are there actually found within the Limits of your Parish, Township, or Place, *at the Time of taking this Account*, distinguishing Males and Females, and *exclusive* of Men actually serving in His Majesty's Regular Forces, the Old Militia, or in any *Embodied* Local Militia, and *exclusive* of Seamen either in His Majesty's Service or belonging to Registered Vessels?
6. Referring to the Number of Persons in 1801, To what Cause do you attribute any remarkable Difference in the Number at present?
7. Are there any other Matters, which you may think it necessary to remark, in Explanation of your Answers to any of the preceding Questions?

1971

The head of each household had to provide the following information for each resident.

Age, sex, marital condition, relationship to head of household, usual residence; country of birth, country of birth of each person's father and mother (new question); address one year ago, address five years ago; date of first marriage and termination of that marriage (women under 60 only); dates of birth of all children born alive to such women in marriage (new question); occupation, industry and place of work, description of work done, occupation one year ago, normal hours of work: educational qualifications equivalent to 'A' level and above.

Housing tenure, number of rooms, number of cars, degree of sharing with other householders, shared or exclusive use of cookers, sinks, fixed baths, hot water supplies, inside or outside toilets.

Residents who were absent on census night.

It's a big form with a big job to do

There are a lot of questions on the Census form—more than ever before. Some may seem trivial. But when all the answers from all the forms are put together and sorted out, they add up to something really valuable. They form the sound basis for all sorts of research and planning. For instance, by comparing these results with previous Censuses we can see the way we have been developing—and get a good idea which way we are likely to go in future. Or we can check the results against facts from other sources—sickness or accident figures, for example — to get a new insight into many important problems.

More housing

Looking to the future

Schools for t

The jobs we

Part of the propaganda explaining the need for the 1971 census.

The lists of questions show how the amount of census information gathered in both England and the United States has increased over the years. The first census in England in 1801 was little more than a count of heads by the local overseer and it was not until 1841 that entries were made by name. Compare this with the mass of information gathered by the 1971 census

Better health

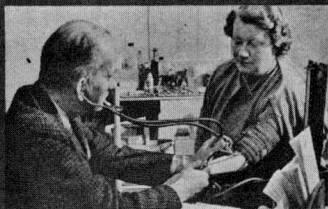

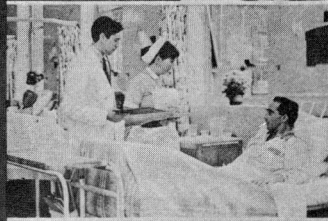

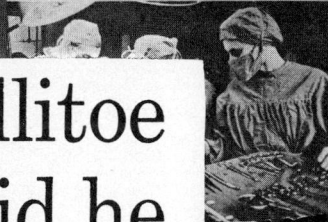

Sillitoe said he was 101

Mr Alan Sillitoe, the writer, gave his age as 101 on his census form last April. His real age is 43, and yesterday at Ashford, Kent, he was fined £25 with £10 costs for not filling in the form properly.

Mr Sillitoe, of Wittersham, near Rye, filled in only the names of his wife, Ruth Fainlight, the poet, his two children, and himself. He left the rest of the form blank. He pleaded guilty and he told the court: " This census form was an interrogation on paper, not a mere counting of heads. The information seemed far in excess of what ought to have been given."

He said after the hearing: "Anyone who could afford to pay the fine but who filled in the form must have the soul of a slave."

The census in 1971 asked for more information than any previous census. Some felt that the census

US Census questions

1790

Name of family head; free white males of 16 years and up. free white males under 16; free white females; slaves; other persons.

1880

Address; name; relationship to family head; sex; race; age; marital status; month of birth if born within the census year; married within the year; occupation; months unemployed during year; sickness or temporary disability; whether blind, deaf and dumb, idiotic, insane, maimed, crippled, bedridden, or otherwise disabled; school attendance; literacy; birthplace of person and parents.

Supplemental schedules for the Indian population; for persons who died during the year; insane; idiots; deaf-mutes; blind; homeless children; prisoners; paupers and indigent persons.

1970

Population

Information obtained for all persons: Address; name; relationship to household head; sex; race; age; marital status.

Information obtained for 20-percent sample: Birthplace; educational attainment; for women, number of children ever born; employment status; hours worked in week; year last worked; occupation, industry, and class of worker; activity five years ago; weeks worked last year; income last year; location of residence five years ago.

Information obtained for 15-percent sample: Country of birth of parents; length of residence at present address; language spoken in childhood home; school attendance; veteran status; location of place of work; means of transportation to work.

Information obtained for 5-percent sample: If foreign born, whether naturalized, and year of immigration; whether married more than once, date of first marriage, and whether first marriage ended because of death of spouse; vocational training; for persons of working age, presence and duration of disability; occupation, industry, and class of worker five years ago.

Housing

Information obtained for all housing units: Occupied or vacant; owned, rented, or no cash rent; if vacant, vacancy status (for sale, for rent, etc.) and duration of vacancy; number of units at this address; single or multiple family structure; trailers; number of rooms; basement; access to unit; water supply; toilet facilities; bathing facilities; kitchen facilities; telephone available; value or contract rent.

Information obtained for 20-percent sample: Whether on a farm; year built; number of units in structure; gross rent; heating equipment.

Information obtained for 15-percent sample: Number of bathrooms; source of water; sewage disposal; air conditioning; automobiles.

Information obtained for 5-percent sample: Number of bedrooms; number of stories; elevators; heating fuel; cooking fuel; water heating fuel; battery-operated radio sets; clothes washing machines; clothes dryers; home food freezers; television sets; dishwashers; second homes.

A historical study of population

One of the most famous studies of population history is by the American biologist, Edward S. Deevey. His table of population growth shows that man first appeared (probably in Africa) about one million years ago. By studying the population density of modern hunting and food-gathering people such as the Australian Aborigines, Deevey calculated that by 10 000 BC, when man had probably spread to all continents, there were about five million people occupying the habitable land space. When man had discovered how to select and cultivate various kinds of grasses, roots and fruit trees, and how to domesticate animals,

the population began to grow more rapidly until it had passed one hundred million by the time of Christ. There was another surge of population at the time of the Industrial Revolution in the seventeenth and eighteenth centuries when the world population shot up from five hundred million to over three thousand million. The rate of population growth at the moment is so high that it is almost certain to *double* between now and the end of the century.

Estimated world populations, and population densities in persons per square kilometre (after Deevey, 1960).

Years ago	Population	Density
1 000 000	125 000	0·00425
300 000	1 000 000	0.012
25 000	3 340 000	0·04
10 000	5 320 000	0·04
6000	86 500 000	1·0
2000	133 000 000	1·0
310	545 000 000	3·7
210	728 000 000	4·9
160	906 000 000	6·2
60	1 610 000 000	11·0
10	2 400 000 000	16·4

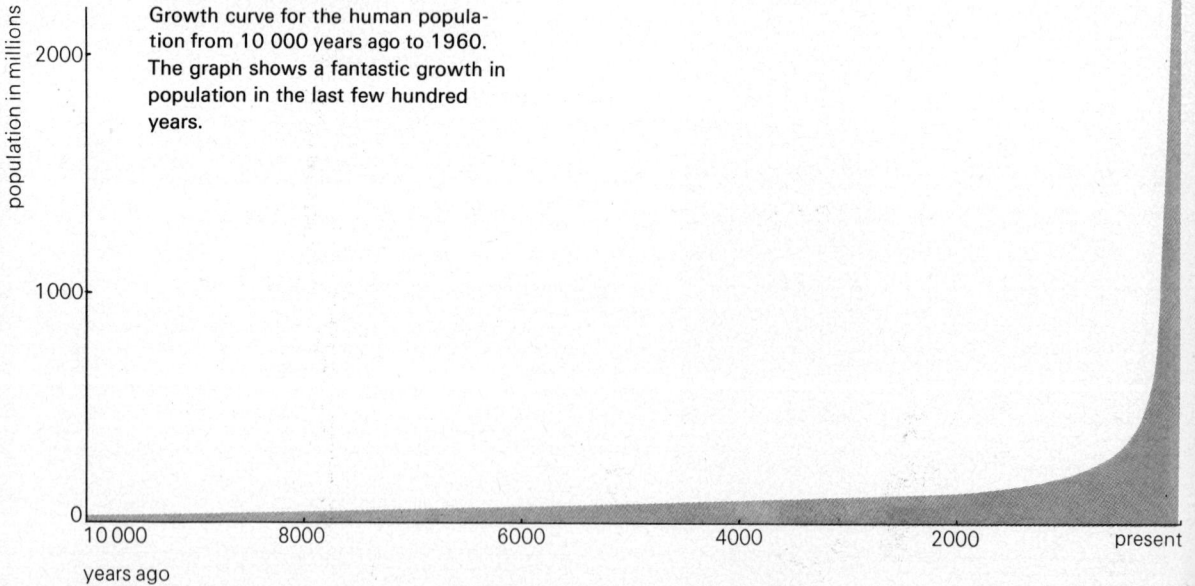

Growth curve for the human population from 10 000 years ago to 1960. The graph shows a fantastic growth in population in the last few hundred years.

Causes of population increase

The human population differs from that of other species in that it can change its methods of food production quite quickly. It has done this on two occasions in history, namely, the Agricultural and Industrial Revolutions, and each was followed by a surge of population growth. One reason for the sudden increase after the Agricultural Revolution could be the change in man's diet from one which consisted mainly of hunted animals, to a diet with more plants in it.

Suppose that the men in one area lived by killing and eating buffaloes, and the buffaloes in turn lived by eating the grass. Only one-tenth of the energy from the grass eaten is stored in the buffalo as meat, so that if the men could somehow bypass the buffalo and live on the grass in the area, they ought to be able to get ten times as much food energy. When the men started to farm, this would become at least partially possible, since the staple diet would consist of specially prepared and cooked grass seeds, perhaps in the form of bread. The food in the same area could now support several times the original population.

About ten thousand years later, the scientific–industrial revolution brought chemical, biological and mechanical improvements in farming. This increased productivity of the farms opened the way to another large increase in the human population.

Of course the Agricultural and Industrial Revolutions did not happen suddenly, at the same time, all over the world. The Australian Aborigines are an example of a people still living at the hunting and food-gathering stage typical of the Stone-Age man. An example of the early stages of the Agricultural Revolution occurs in South America, where tribes of

A projection of world population growth to the year 2000. The shaded band shows the most likely range if the population continues to grow in the same way it does at the moment. The prospects for the poor and under-developed areas of the world are particularly frightening.

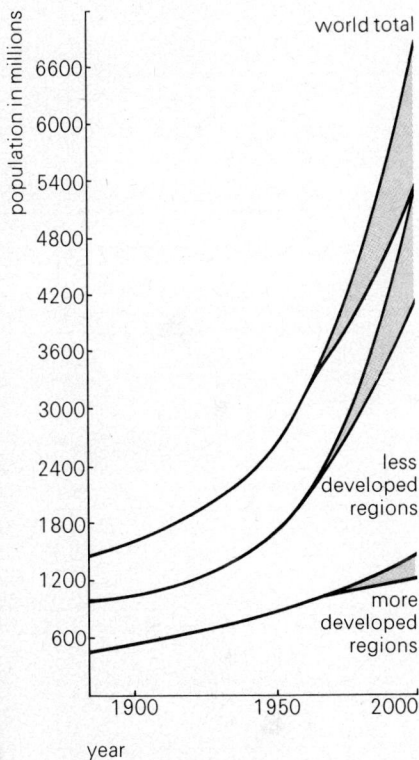

population in millions

6600
6000
5400
4800
4200
3600
3000
2400
1800
1200
600

world total

less developed regions

more developed regions

1900   1950   2000

year

The Wai-Wai Indians live in South America and grow their crops in specially cleared areas of the forest. Here they are using long digging-sticks to plant silk grass, used in making rope and string. In a short time the soil will be exhausted and the indians will have to move and clear another area of forest.

Indians live by 'nomadic garden culture'. They plant a cleared area in the forest, harvest it, and then move on to somewhere else. They have no knowledge of fertilizers or the rotation of crops, so after each crop the land is exhausted, and they are forced to move on. The existence of such groups of people enables us to make fairly informed guesses about the probable number of people living in ancient communities. We start by assuming that the density of modern populations depends on their stage of cultural evolution. We then relate this back to other regions in prehistoric times which had similar methods of food production. From the area of the land occupied, it is possible to calculate a theoretical size for the population. There are snags in this way of estimating numbers, of course. The climate over much of Australia is very different from that in Europe when it was inhabited by tribesmen from the Old Stone Age. Consequently, the two regions had quite different amounts of plant life. Plants are the 'producers' from which all animals live either directly or indirectly. Because the favourable climate of Stone-Age Europe could support many more plants than the hot, dry Australian bush where the Aborigines live, more people could live on a unit of European land. Factors of this sort make calculations of the size of ancient populations very complicated.

Population stability

Tribes of traditional peoples in existence today often seem to have stayed the same size for many years. This supports the idea that in past ages the world population stayed at much the same level for many thousands of years. Deevey thinks that, following the spurt in growth-rate started by the Agricultural Revolution, there was a stabilization at a new, higher population level. If this is true, it suggests that the human-population growth curve has in the past been sigmoid (or S-shaped), like the laboratory population of yeast cells we discussed at the beginning of the chapter. However, Deevey's graph also shows the staggering rate at which the human population is growing at the moment. What will the graph show in the next few hundred years? Does the present growth-rate represent the rising part of a sigmoid curve which will flatten out fairly soon? Or might it be something more disastrous, and represent a continually accelerating growth-rate which, when it reaches a maximum at some future date, will be followed by a 'crash' involving the destruction of thousands of millions of people due to starvation, epidemic disease or stress caused by overcrowding? Estimates of when this date might be vary from the optimism of the Oxford economist Colin Clark, who sees a very long future for mankind, to the estimate of Paul Ehrlich, who sees it coming before the end of this century.

Since we are able to think about our future and plan for it, we ought to be able to prevent a catastrophe due to overpopulation. However, although it seems possible that *in theory* we could feed everybody and, again, *in theory* we could launch massive programmes to slow down the rapid increase in populations, it seems most unlikely that Western nations will accept the lower standards which it will mean for them. People are becoming more and more interested in the way population size is controlled, as well as in ways of improving the use of land and distributing the world's resources fairly. We shall now examine biological aspects of population control, including birth-rate, death-rate, migration and family planning.

Woman gives birth to NINE

SYDNEY, Sunday.
A 29-YEAR-OLD Australian woman gave birth to nine babies in the Royal Hospital for Women in Sydney today.

A hospital spokesman said seven of the tiny babies were alive and had been placed in incubators.

The mother, who was identified as Mrs. Geraldine Brodrick, of Canberra, was reported in a "satisfactory" condition.

It is believed to be the first substantiated report of nine babies being born in one birth.

There is one confirmed case of live-born octuplets — eight babies—born in Mexico City in 1967. But they all died within 14 hours.

The seven surviving babies are three boys and four girls. They were described by the spokesman as "very immature."

The other two—both boys—were still-born.

Mrs. Brodrick went into labour yesterday afternoon.

Australian medical authorities said they believed the births to be the biggest multiple births in history.

Mrs. Brodrick, wife of a Canberra butcher, had been under fertility treatment.

The Brodricks also have two daughters, aged four and five.

3 more wonder babes die

Concern grows for survivors

From JOCK VEITCH in Sydney

ANOTHER three babies of the world's first recorded nonuplet birth died early today.

The three—two boys' and a girl—had earlier suffered breathing difficulties.

And the condition of three of the surviving four, two girls and a boy, is causing concern.

NINTH BABY DIES

SYDNEY, Sunday.—The last survivor of the nine Brodrick babies, born a week ago, has died at Sydney's Royal Hospital for Women, doctors said early today.

A TRAGEDY OF NINE BABIES

by Anne Edwards

THE questions must be asked : Have we allowed the scientists to go too far ? Have we given them too much licence to move in and take over our lives ? Have we permitted them, by default, to become the arbiters not only of life and death, but of the very quality of life ?

A woman will normally have only one child at a time, although multiple births (twins, etc) do occur sometimes. Some women seem incapable of having any children and doctors have developed a fertility drug which has helped many of them to have children. But there have been some tragic examples of multiple births with this drug.

2 Fertility

One of the Pharaohs of Egypt is supposed to have had more than one thousand children, and another Eastern ruler boasted of an eight hundred strong cavalry that were all his own sons. Although these may be exaggerations, there is no doubt that one man can father many more children than one woman can bear.

It is possible to work out the maximum number of children a woman could, in theory, produce. If she became able to bear children when she was fourteen years old and then had one child every ten months until she was forty-five, she would have produced thirty-seven offspring. Very occasionally, cases are reported where a woman has had a very large number of children and we could say of such a person that she had approached her *fecundity*. Fecundity, strictly, is the number of fertile eggs the female produces. Usually, it is taken to mean the number of children a woman could have if she reproduced continuously throughout her fertile life. When we talk of the actual number of children a woman produces, rather than the number she could in theory give birth to, we are describing her *fertility*. Even in countries with very high birth-rates, average fertility is always very much lower than fecundity.

We normally measure birth-rates in terms of the numbers of live births per year per thousand people in the population. This is a very rough-and-ready method because not everybody in the population will have children – for example, none of the men and, in general, none of the women under the age of about ten or over the age of about fifty. However, for measurements on a world scale, this *crude birth-rate* has to do, because there are no figures for *specific birth-rates*, that is, measurements of the birth-rate in a particular group such as women between ten and fifty years of age.

Queen Victoria's family was by no means large for the time. She is pictured here with her nine children and a number of other relatives.

Biological control of population increase

If you look at how long it takes for a newly produced organism to produce another one (this is called the *generation time*), you find that, in general, the larger the organism, the longer the time. Bacteria may reproduce about twenty minutes after they themselves were produced, but elephants must live for twenty years before they are sexually mature and capable of having young. Another difference between species is the number of young they produce at a time. For example, a large female cod may produce four million eggs (potential young) at a time, while humans generally have only one baby at a time. If a woman has quins, it is international news.

In fact, man is one of the least productive animals in terms of numbers of offspring. This is probably because human babies can survive better than other young animals. There are two main reasons for this. Firstly, human babies are relatively large animals and, the larger an animal is, the more independent it is of its environment. If the amount of moisture in the air changes suddenly, or if the concentration of dissolved substances in a solution alters, this may have a catastrophic effect on small organisms living there, whilst larger animals in the same environment may not even notice that there has been a change. Man and the other large mammals are living in a world which is much more friendly than the world occupied by bacteria and protozoa (single-celled animals). In addition, the earliest part of human growth takes place in the uterus of the mother, and therefore an unborn baby has a much safer environment than have, say, cod eggs which are produced in millions by each female and, of which, only one or two are likely to survive.

Maternities with multiple births for women of all ages England and Wales 1969

type	births
twins	8259
triplets	79
quadruplets	1
quintuplets	1
sextuplets	1
total births	797 538

Hunger increases the birth-rate

The reproductive rate of man seems to be affected by how well he eats, but there is disagreement as to whether lack of food increases or decreases the rate.

Josue de Castro, who was Chairman of FAO (the Food and Agriculture Organization of the United Nations) from 1951 to 1955, thought that hunger tended to bring about overpopulation because those countries which have the worst-fed people, such as India, Egypt and various Central American states, are also those showing the most violent increases in population. On the other hand, countries where most people have plenty to eat show a very low rate of population increase, or even a decline. De Castro said that hunger, whilst causing a higher death-rate, increases the birth-rate still further. He suggested that, whenever a species is in danger of dying out (for example, due to starvation), an inbuilt mechanism causes an increase in fertility so that the species will be preserved. To support his opinion, he quoted the results of some experiments on rats. Rats fed on a high-protein diet were less fertile than rats fed on a low-protein diet. They had fewer litters, and fewer young per litter.

Percentage protein in food	Percentage sterile male rats	Percentage sterile female rats
10	5	6
18	22	23
22	40	38

At the same time, the health and survival rate of the well-fed rats and their offspring was much better, so that on balance they maintained their population size as well as the rats on the low-protein diet. This balancing off is sometimes called a homeostatic (staying the same) effect.

De Castro explained what happened as follows. Fertility depends partly on the secretion of hormones called oestrogens, and when excess oestrogens are secreted, they are carried in the blood stream to the liver, where they are broken down. But people suffering from protein deficiency often have fatty degeneration of the liver. Therefore the liver is less efficient at destroying excess oestrogens, and consequently these people are more fertile.

Average number of offspring per year.

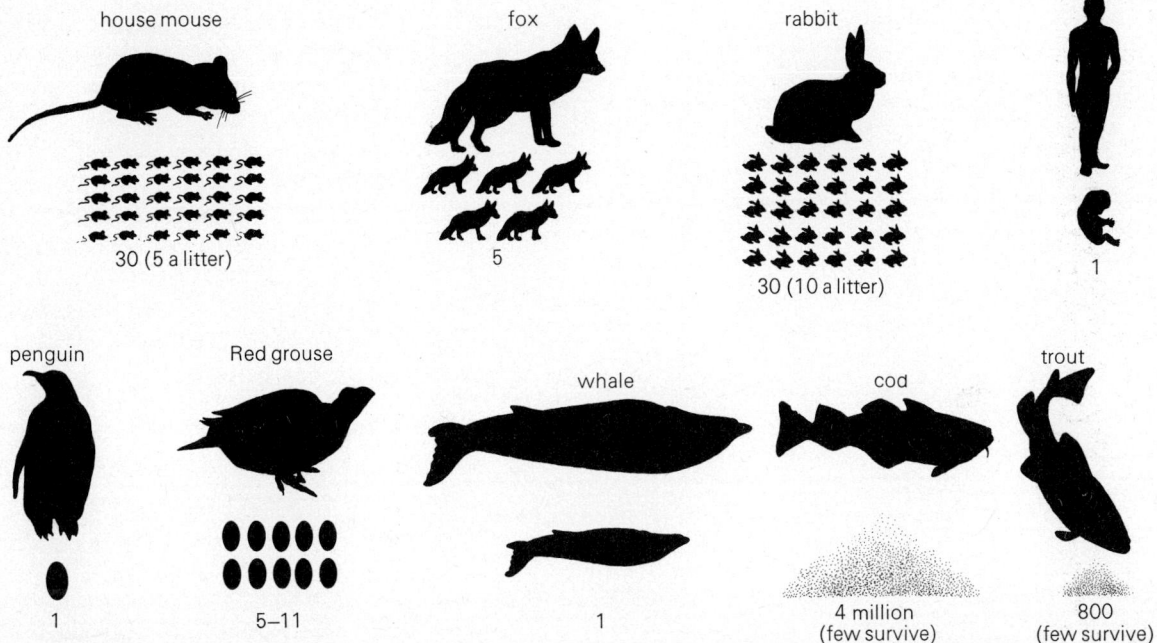

house mouse

fox

rabbit

man

30 (5 a litter)

5

30 (10 a litter)

1

penguin

Red grouse

whale

cod

trout

1

5–11

1

4 million
(few survive)

800
(few survive)

Hunger decreases the birth-rate

The argument by de Castro is not very popular today, because there is so much evidence in support of the opposite idea, that fertility is increased with better nutrition. Dr John Hammond of the Cambridge School of Agriculture pointed out that well-fed farm animals mature earlier, have a larger number of successful breeding seasons, shed more eggs at ovulation and have a higher survival rate for fertilized eggs than do poorly fed animals. The same seems true for man.

During a severe famine in Madras in 1877, relief workers kept records, and found that although over one hundred thousand people were being cared for in emergency camps, only thirty-nine births were recorded. Nine months after the worst food shortage was over the birth-rate was only four to five per thousand as compared with the usual rate of twenty-nine per thousand in the same district. Again, under the starvation conditions existing in German concentration camps during the Second World War, it was commonly recorded that women stopped menstruating, although this may have been due to stress rather than simply food shortage.

During the last war Ancel Keys studied the effects of starvation on a group of conscientious objectors. Among other things, he discovered that the starvation of men caused the numbers of sperms in the seminal fluid to drop to levels which made the men sterile. Recovery of fertility after the end of the starvation regime took about twenty weeks. The volunteers also mentioned that they lost interest in the opposite sex, and had a constant craving for food.

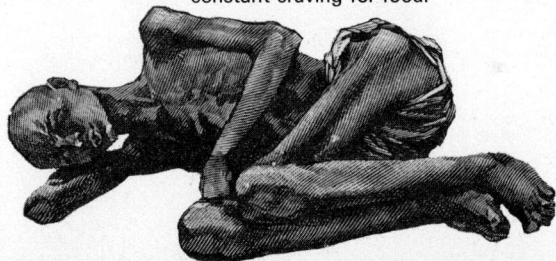

Annual increase in population as a percentage of the total population for selected countries

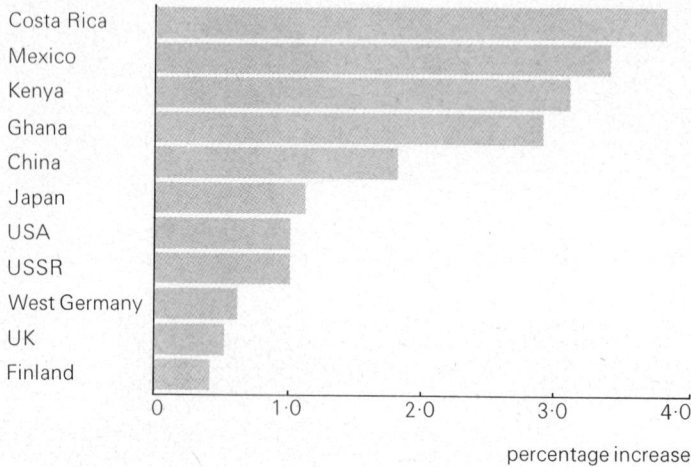

Costa Rica				
Mexico				
Kenya				
Ghana				
China				
Japan				
USA				
USSR				
West Germany				
UK				
Finland				

0   1·0   2·0   3·0   4·0

percentage increase

Crude birth rates per 1000 population for selected countries

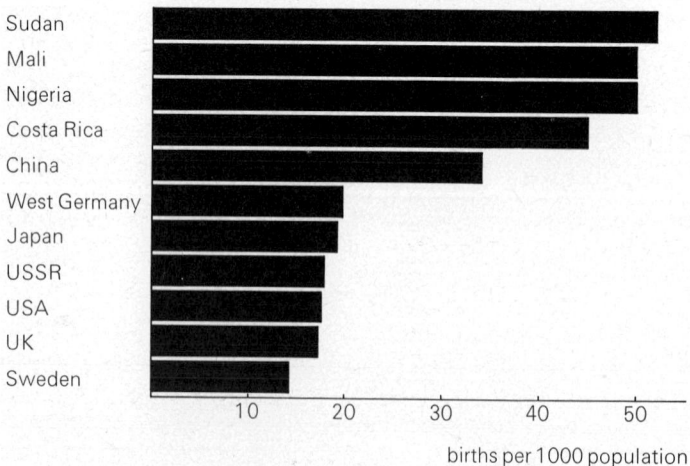

Sudan	
Mali	
Nigeria	
Costa Rica	
China	
West Germany	
Japan	
USSR	
USA	
UK	
Sweden	

10   20   30   40   50

births per 1000 population

Social factors affecting fertility

In Asia, Africa and Latin America, birth-rates are commonly above thirty-five per thousand, and in certain areas, such as Guinea and Mali in West Africa, they are probably as high as fifty to fifty-five per thousand. In North America, Europe and the Soviet Union, the birth-rate is usually below twenty-five per thousand, and the richer, better-fed people often have smaller families than the poor. This seems to contradict the biological evidence we have just discussed, and there may be other social factors related to low fertility, with perhaps a common link.

Urbanization

After the Industrial Revolution, all Western nations showed a drop in fertility. People living in the country in most European states have had higher birth-rates than city dwellers for at least a century. In the United States it has even been shown that the larger the city, the less fertile are its inhabitants. However, in recent years the fertility gap between rural and city dwellers has been narrowing, and country people are having fewer children than they used to.

Social mobility

People who become rich and move up the social scale usually have fewer children than those who are less successful. Sir Ronald Fisher once argued that since people with few children were more likely to succeed, the upper classes ought gradually to consist of people with below-average fecundity.

Standard of living

In fact the largest families are often found at opposite ends of the social scale, amongst the very rich and the very poor.

Family groups

A Victorian family.

The extended family
of a Bushman.

The 'ideal' Western family.

Status of women

There is some evidence that, in societies where women have become more emancipated, there has been a drop in the birth-rate. The relatively low density of the population in Burma compared with neighbouring India is said to be related to the higher status of Burmese women.

Religion

There are differences in the fertility of different religious groups. For instance, in countries inhabited by Europeans, Catholics have the highest fertility, Protestants next and Jews the lowest fertility. There is also evidence that people who are very religious tend to have more children than those who are less religious.

Bad economic conditions

If you compare the birth-rates for whole nations at different times, there often seems to be a fall in the birth-rate when economic conditions become difficult. During the Depression of the 1930s, the birth-rate in the United States dropped from 21·3 in 1930 to 18·7 in 1935, and it rose to 19·4 in 1940.

Today it is generally agreed that the common factor linking all these cases is not biological, but social. It is the practice of birth-control.

People have used various methods of contraception for thousands of years, but it is only in recent history that contraceptive devices and the pill have been widely regarded as socially or morally acceptable, and therefore easily available. People in cities are likely to know about them before country people; well-educated people are also better informed; however, there may be opposition to contraceptives on religious grounds. So, people who are socially ambitious or well-educated usually have the information necessary to limit their families by means of contraception.

High and low fertility

We have seen that, in general, people in the rich countries of the world have low birth-rates and those in the poor countries have high birth-rates. However, there has not always been this difference between advanced and underdeveloped parts of the world. This becomes clear if you look at the graph showing the birth-rates for Sweden between 1750 and 1935. Early on the birth-rates are round about forty per thousand, that is, well within the range typical of an underdeveloped area. By 1930 the figure had dropped to the region of fifteen per thousand,

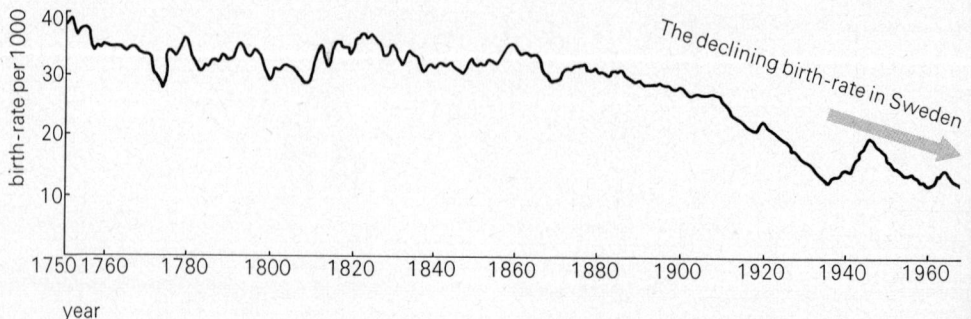

The declining birth-rate in Sweden

with the most obvious drop at the end of the nineteenth century. From the latter part of the nineteenth century to the 1930s, the birth-rate had dropped by almost two-thirds. We do not have such detailed figures for other countries but the Swedish pattern seems to be typical of other Western countries (except France, where the decline set in earlier).

It is important to remember that what is being discussed here is the 'crude' birth-rate, that is, the figure is taken over the whole population, whether or not they are capable of producing children. Western-type populations contain large numbers of middle-aged and old people, but in countries with high fertility the majority of people are young. In these countries, a large proportion of the population is able to have children.

In addition, various other biological factors may have an effect on fertility. There is some evidence that a high environmental temperature reduces fertility, perhaps by preventing spermatozoa from maturing. Men whose testicles did not come down into the scrotum out of the abdomen are infertile because the temperature inside the abdomen is too high to allow the germ cells to develop. The length of the day affects the mating behaviour of many animals and there may be a connection between the amount of exposure to sunlight and fertility in man. Finally, some people think that more births occur during the new and full phases of the moon than at other times. However, the existence of these biological factors is rather speculative and they are less important than social factors in controlling fertility.

Mr and Mrs Harrison with their family of 13 boys.

A children's cemetery in Santiago, Chile. In 1965 over 10 per cent of all children born in Chile died before reaching their first birthday. Chile has the highest infant mortality rate in South America.

3 Mortality

Longevity

At Cape Verde on the West African Coast, there are baobab trees which were already a thousand years old when Moses led the children of Israel out of Egypt. These trees can be up to nine metres in diameter, and people often hollow out the trunk of a living tree and use it as a house. Trees in general last longer than other living things, but this is due to the mechanical resistance of the dead heart wood as much as to the living parts of the tree.

In animals, the life-span is seldom more than one hundred years. There are records of two species of tortoise living for more than one hundred years, but amongst the mammals, man holds the record. Elephants come next with a maximum recorded age of sixty-seven years, bears live for thirty years and lions for twenty. These are maximum figures for animals living in zoos; in normal circumstances most animals die well before this because they are either killed and eaten by predators, or die from disease or accidents.

Traditionally, men are supposed to live for three score years and ten but only recently has the average figure been near this. Studies of Greek skeletons dug up in ancient cemeteries show that their average age varied from about thirty years in the early Bronze Age to about forty years two thousand years ago. Egyptian mummies are the bodies of people who died on average at twenty-two years old. In ancient Rome the average age at death was twenty years, although people living in Roman North Africa could expect to live up to fifty years.

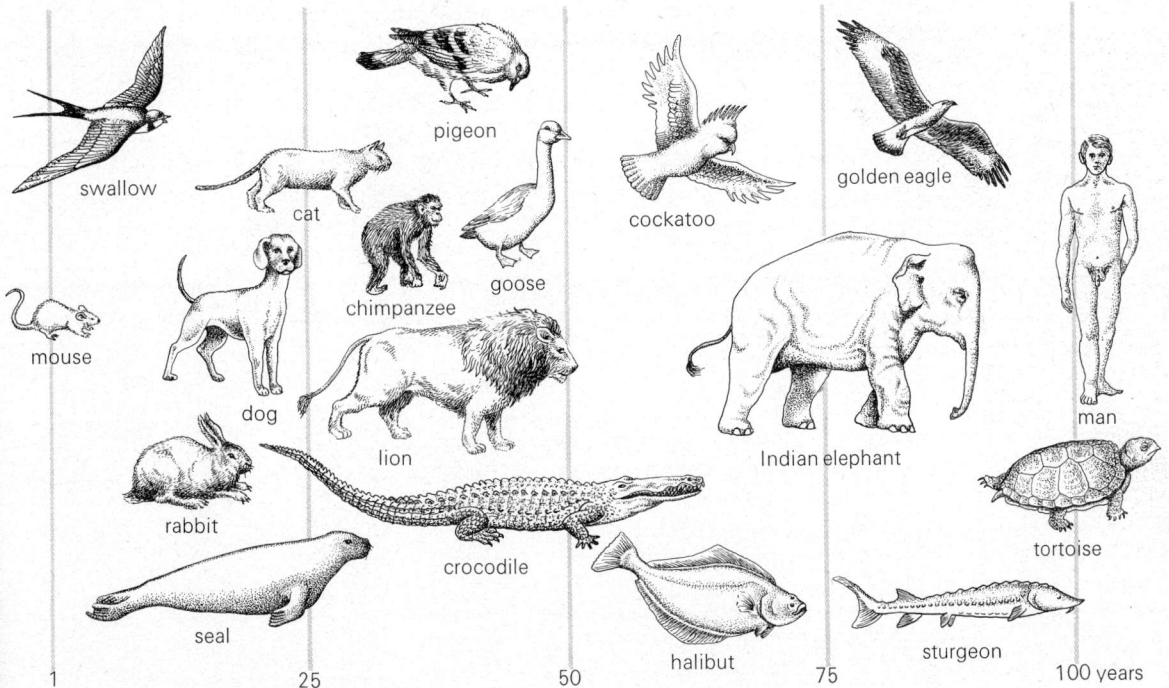

swallow

pigeon

cat

cockatoo

golden eagle

chimpanzee

goose

mouse

dog

lion

Indian elephant

man

rabbit

crocodile

tortoise

seal

halibut

sturgeon

1   25   50   75   100 years

The life span of some animals.

The picture is much the same for most of the two thousand years after that, and even by the end of the nineteenth century the new-born Briton could not hope to live much longer than someone from Roman Africa. There are records of notable exceptions. For example, a Dane called Christen Drakenberg was said to have been born in 1626, married at the age of one hundred and eleven and died when he was one hundred and forty-six years old. Do you believe this?

Even with the greatest advances in disease prevention, almost everybody would probably die before the age of one hundred and ten.

There are new drugs which are said to lengthen the normal life-span of rats and mice. It is too early to say what effects these may have on man. Many biologists think there are advantages in having a particular length of life and that the natural life-spans of different species are the result of evolution. Normally, mammals do not die immediately after having reached sexual maturity, nor do they live for ever. Presumably, then, a balance has been achieved between the advantages of a long and a short life. A short life-span means that there will be a quick turn-over of generations, so any valuable genetic variations in shape or form can spread

Life expectancy

In nature, very few animals die of old age. They are usually killed or eaten by other animals, or catch a disease or have an accident before growing old. Different species of animals vary in their patterns of survival and one way of showing this is to work out a set of *survivorship curves*. Suppose that we were able to watch a large group of animals of the same species from the moment of their birth until the point where the last member of the group had died. We can plot the number of survivors at each point in time, and the graph will probably resemble one of the four survivorship curves shown here.

In ancient Rome, and in some modern underdeveloped countries, man probably had a type III survivorship curve (with people dying off regularly throughout the normal life-span) similar to that of many birds. But in industrial nations the curve is much more like type I for the starved fruit flies. Most people live out their allotted span, then die.

Type I curves are produced in cases when all individuals survive to the physiological limit and then all die at the same time. This is very unusual in nature but it can be obtained for a population of fruit flies hatched out together and then kept without food until they all starve to death.

Type II, where there is a constant number of deaths per unit of time, is found in populations of hydra.

Type III, where a constant proportion of the population die per unit of time, is found, for example, in several species of birds.

Type IV curves are for populations which produce very large numbers of young, most of which die in the early stages of development. Fish are the best examples of this type.

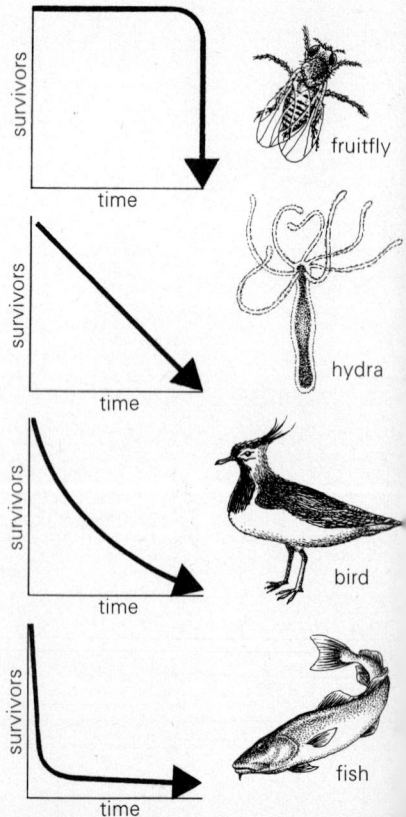

fruitfly

hydra

bird

fish

through the population quickly. Because of this the species can exploit a rapidly changing environment, as favourable variations fit the young animals for the new conditions. Also, in a good year a dense population can grow quickly, and subside in the following year if conditions are bad. A slow-growing species cannot make use of this brief opportunity. On the other hand, a long life allows an animal to grow to a large size, which in turn permits it to become more independent of changes in the environment. In addition, the fact that a long-lived animal has a number of successive breeding seasons means that the species can survive even after a disastrous year when all the young die.

Man can pass on, from generation to generation, instructions and advice on how to do things: how to light fires, make tools, where to find food, continue long-term projects, etc. Each new individual does not have to start from scratch. The resulting build-up of knowledge over the centuries helps the species to survive in very hostile environments. He can survive on the moon's surface where no other organism could remain alive. Natural selection has favoured a long life-span because older people pass on valuable advice to the group.

Males		Age	Females	
l_x	$°e_x$	x	l_x	$°e_x$
10,000	68.5	0	10,000	74.8
9,797	68.9	1	9,844	75.0
9,783	68.0	2	9,832	74.1
9,774	67.1	3	9,826	73.2
9,769	66.1	4	9,822	72.2
9,763	65.2	5	9,818	71.2
9,742	60.3	10	9,806	66.3
9,724	55.4	15	9,795	61.4
9,679	50.6	20	9,776	56.5
9,634	45.9	25	9,755	51.6
9,590	41.1	30	9,729	46.8
9,538	36.3	35	9,694	41.9
9,463	31.6	40	9,635	37.2
9,322	27.0	45	9,528	32.5
9,066	22.7	50	9,362	28.1
8,654	18.6	55	9,113	23.8
7,985	15.0	60	8,745	19.7
6,946	11.9	65	8,191	15.6
5,523	9.3	70	7,337	12.4
3,870	7.2	75	6,102	9.4
2,289	5.4	80	4,470	6.9
1,030	4.0	85	2,646	4.9

Life table

Another way of expressing this is to draw up a life table like those published every year by the Central Statistical Office. By reading across the table you can find the probable life expectancy for each age group in the British population ($°e_x$) as well as the number of people who would survive to a given age out of an original sample of 10 000 (l_x). Babies under one year old do not have as great a life expectancy as children between one and five years. This produces a dip at the beginning of the human survivorship curve. Infant mortality in some parts of the world such as Guinea, Niger, Zambia and Gabon is more than two hundred per thousand. In Western Europe it ranges from 12·8 in Norway, to about thirty per thousand in some other countries. In Britain in the 1960s, it varied between about nineteen in England to 26·5 in Northern Ireland.

A life-table from the Abridged Life Tables for 1969.

A food-chain pyramid is a method of showing how creatures depend on each other for food. Although this pyramid is a simplification of a very complex food-web, it shows clearly that a change in the number of creatures in any layer will affect the other layers.

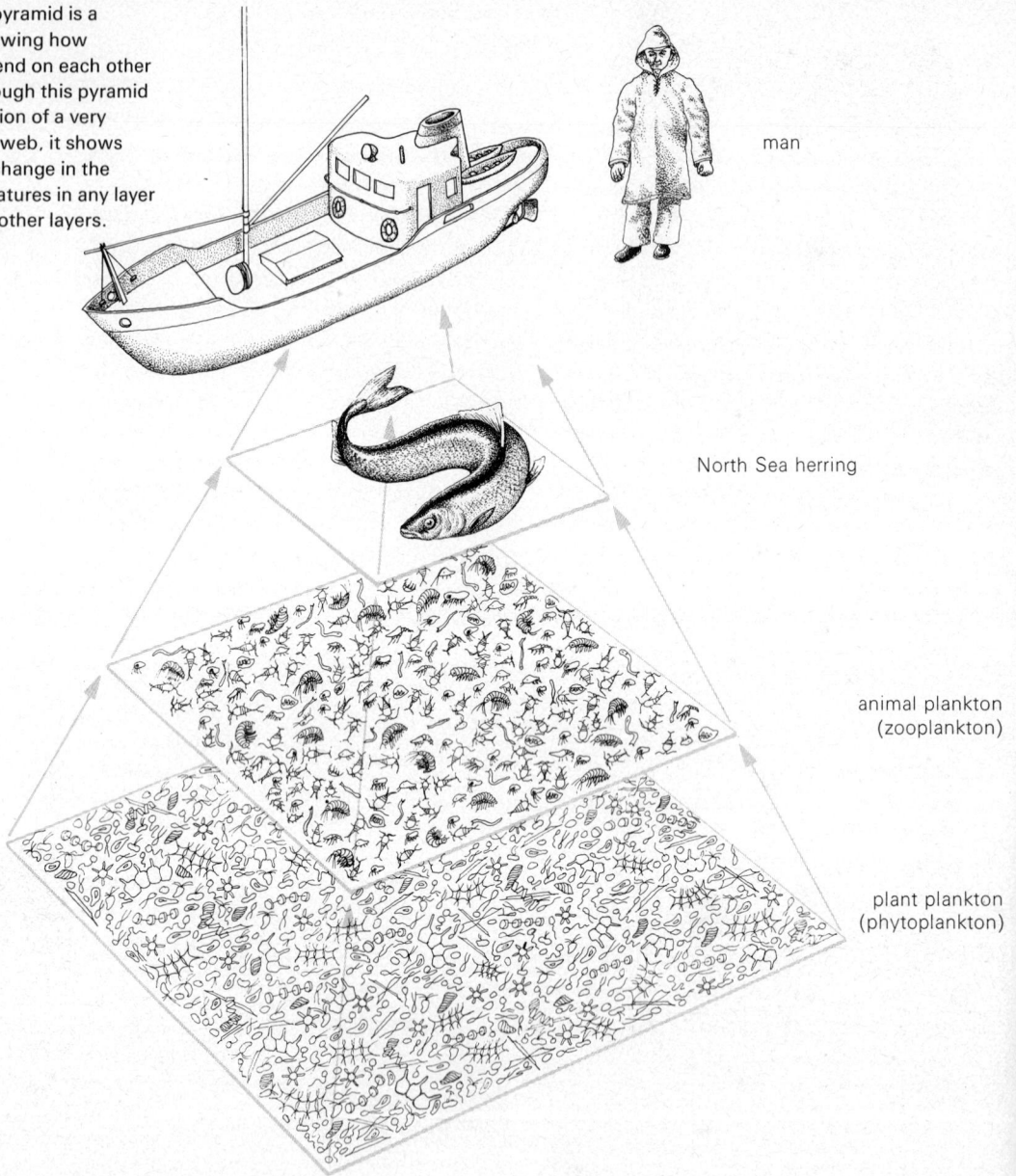

man

North Sea herring

animal plankton (zooplankton)

plant plankton (phytoplankton)

Causes of death

Being eaten by another animal is probably the most frequent cause of death among animals in general, because they are usually a link in a food chain in which each member of the chain depends on the member below for its food. Only what are called 'top predators' such as lions, hawks, crocodiles and man normally escape, but even their young may form the prey of some animals. But probably this was never an important cause of death in man.

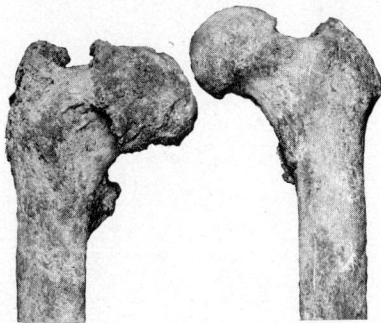

The main cause of man's death has always been disease. We see from the remains of men from the Old Stone Age (Paleolithic) that illnesses such as tuberculosis and arthritis were common then. Contagious diseases were probably not as important in prehistoric times as in later history, because population densities were so low that diseases would rarely reach epidemic proportions.

On the other hand, during historical times epidemic diseases have caused spectacular destruction. In 1348 the great plague first appeared in Central Europe, where it is claimed to have killed a quarter of the population. The cause was a bacterium which passed into the human blood-stream when a man was bitten by an infected rat-flea. It appeared in two main forms. One was bubonic plague, in which swellings of the lymph nodes cause large lumps or 'buboes' to appear at the hip and shoulder joints; the other was pneumonic plague, which attacks the respiratory system, causing pneumonia. The victim usually died in three to four days. There were further epidemics in 1361, 1371 and 1382, each one being successively less severe. It persisted locally, broke out in the London plague of 1664, and then disappeared. However, plague is still found in parts of Asia, and in 1968 was reported amongst the armed forces in Vietnam. Other killer diseases include smallpox, cholera and typhus, all of which were common in the nineteenth century and have now practically disappeared from Europe. In other parts of the world they still continue to cause many deaths, along with tropical diseases such as malaria, yellow fever and sleeping sickness.

The plague of Naples, 1656.

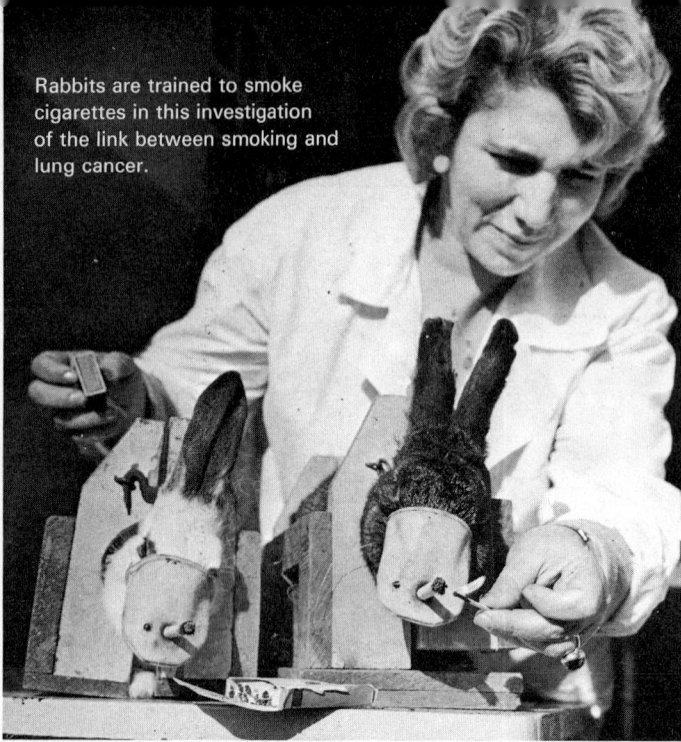

Rabbits are trained to smoke cigarettes in this investigation of the link between smoking and lung cancer.

In industrial nations, cancer, heart disease and various diseases of old age have replaced infectious diseases as the main causes of death. There is now great interest in cancer research, spare-part surgery and the causes of ageing. In the past, epidemic diseases killed most people before degenerative and cancerous conditions appeared.

Famines have occurred very frequently throughout history, especially amongst agricultural people with a population close to the maximum. The most disastrous famines of recent times have been in India, where one and a half million people died in Bengal in 1943, and China. The failure of the potato crop in Ireland in 1845–6 caused the death of between two and three million people. The catastrophes in Biafra in 1969 and in Bangladesh in 1971 are examples of famines resulting from warfare. In this type of famine it is not crop failure but the destruction of food stores or transport systems which causes suffering.

If the energy content of the diet drops much below an average of about 6700 kilojoules per member of the population per day, body weight drops by more than 25 per cent. The drop in body weight reduces the amount of active tissue including, eventually, the heart muscle, which shrinks. This damage to the heart cannot usually be repaired and the person dies. When there is very severe starvation, constant diarrhoea occurs and this is frequently the cause of death. There is often an increase in violence, and cannibalism sometime appears. In most cases the actual cause of death is a disease (and this could be a common disease which does not normally kill) which finds an easy victim in a weakened body.

Accidents and violence taken together are the fourth major cause of *ecological* death (that is, death not due to old age). With one exception, accident rates have not changed much in recent years in industrial countries. The exception is road accidents. To try and cut the number of road accidents, many governments have tightened up safety regulations for the mechanical condition of cars and have tried to discourage drivers from drinking alcohol by introducing breathalyser tests.

The wars in the twentieth century have caused very large numbers of deaths. Approxi-

Ping-ti Ho, who has studied how the population of China changed over the last four hundred years, provides an account of a famine in China which gives a good idea of what they were like:
'In [China in] 1877–8 when four northern provinces were struck [by famine], cannibalism occurred frequently and officials connived at evasion of the laws forbidding sale of children in order to enable parents to buy a few days' food.'

The dead were so numerous that they were interred in 10,000 man holes, and dead children were thrown into water wells. An estimated 9–13 million people perished from hunger, disease and violence.

mately twenty million soldiers and civilians were killed as a direct result of the First World War, and another twenty millions died from famines and epidemics, attributable to the effects of the war. In direct casualties, the Second World War was even worse: twenty-two million people died. Nevertheless, throughout the history of man, warfare has so far had only a temporary effect on population growth. Although during a war the birth-rate goes down and the death-rate goes up, there is a very big rise in the birth-rate once the war is over, and the population quickly returns to its normal level. The large number of children born just after the Second World War in Great Britain was known as the 'bulge' as it filled classrooms to overflowing on its way through the education system. Since the world population is increasing at the rate of seventy million per year, twenty-two million people (the number killed in the Second World War) will be born in less than four months.

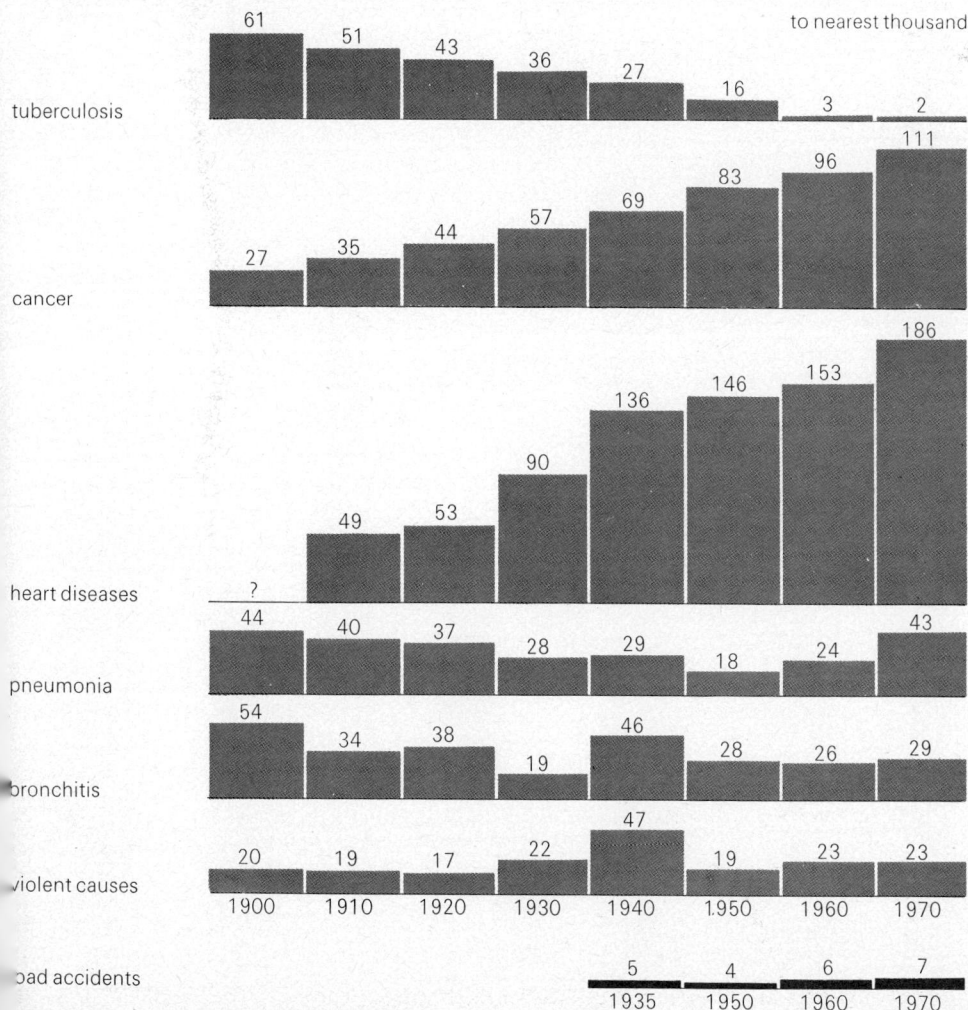

to nearest thousand

tuberculosis: 61 51 43 36 27 16 3 2

cancer: 27 35 44 57 69 83 96 111

heart diseases: ? 49 53 90 136 146 153 186

pneumonia: 44 40 37 28 29 18 24 43

bronchitis: 54 34 38 19 46 28 26 29

violent causes: 20 19 17 22 47 19 23 23

1900 1910 1920 1930 1940 1950 1960 1970

road accidents: 5 (1935) 4 (1950) 6 (1960) 7 (1970)

The changing pattern of disease since 1900.

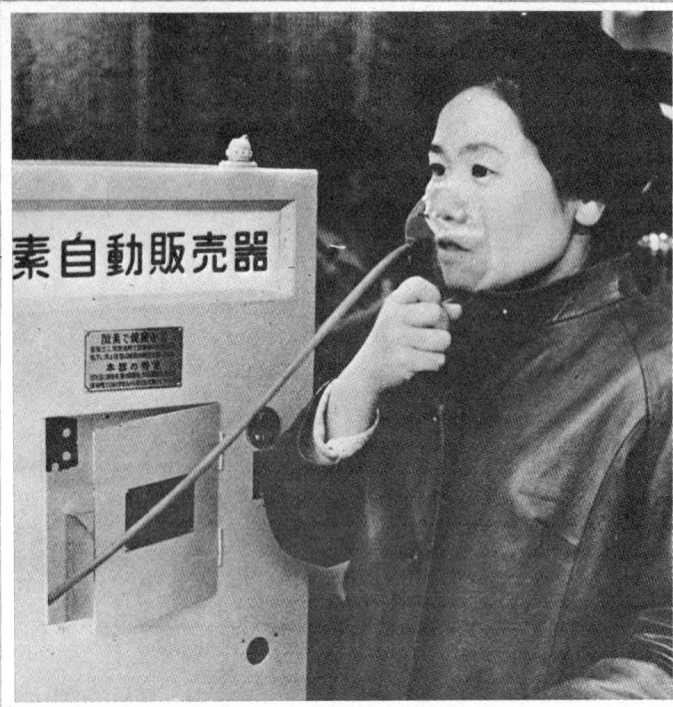

A coin-operated fresh-air machine in Tokyo, Japan. As a result of rapid industrialization Japan has many pollution problems.

Differences in death-rates

Although the maximum life-span for man does not seem to be longer than it used to be, more people are approaching it. In industrial countries this has occurred in three stages. About a hundred years ago there was a major peak in the death-rate in winter and another in mid-summer. The winter peak was due to respiratory infections and the summer peak was partly due to intestinal infections caused by poor sanitation. By the end of the nineteenth century, improved methods for dealing with intestinal infections caused a decline in the summer death-rate, and by about 1950 success in the control of respiratory diseases reduced the winter toll. In big cities like Los Angeles, however, winter can still be a dangerous time

Atmospheric pollution in Dallas, Texas.

because 'smog', caused by polluted atmosphere, increases the chance of respiratory infection. Even before the more recent medical advances, there had been an overall drop in European death-rates, and this was probably due to the increasing standard of living.

High death-rates are found particularly in countries where people have low incomes, high illiteracy (so that they cannot find out how to help themselves), where most people live in the country and where there is a shortage of medical facilities. In countries like this, communicable diseases such as cholera, small-pox and plague still account for a large proportion of deaths. In India all these reach epidemic proportions from time to time and active tuberculosis is permanently widespread.

Modern public health measures sometimes produce an apparently miraculous drop in the death-rate in some areas. In Ceylon, for example, the use of DDT to kill insects which carry diseases such as malaria cut the death-rate from twenty to twelve per thousand in a seven-year period after the Second World War. The most significant drop was in infant deaths, which in this type of area can account for a third of all deaths.

The agonizing problem associated with the type of success described is that, whilst there has been successful death-control in many countries, there is often no corresponding success in birth-control and the population explosion becomes greater still. Some people believe that the solution to the problem is a cruel one, that we should stop trying to cut the death-rate.

Refugees from Bangladesh.

4 Migrations

About twenty years ago, an American biologist, John Emlen, released five pairs of adult mice in a basement store-room in the University of Wisconsin. He hoped to find out what happened as the population increased. Each day he left 250 grams of food for the animals and for a time the mice stayed there. The pairs were breeding, the population began to go up and it eventually reached the point where 250 grams of food was only just enough to feed all the mice. At this point the mice began to leave the store-room and spread all over the building. This migration was a response to the shortage of food.

Emigrations following large increases in populations are common to many species and are usually caused either by food shortage or by overcrowding. Quite often all the animals who emigrate may die, but those left behind survive, so that the migration has served as a means of rapidly reducing population density to a level where there is enough food and space for them all. In general, those animals high in the social hierarchy pressurize those lower down the hierarchy until the population is thinned out to the point where the available food resources are sufficient. The 'pioneers' are usually young animals, forced to move beyond the home area to some more distant spot, thus extending the range of the species.

The first migrations

It is widely believed that the various human races had their origin in one area of the Earth (one idea is that this was in Africa), but by the time history was being written down, men were to be found in all the continents. Because Africa, Asia and Europe form a single land mass, migration from one continent to another

was possible. However, for men venturing towards other land masses there were considerable problems, and there is good evidence that man has only recently come to these places.

Australia had been isolated for a very long time when men first arrived there in the late Pleistocene era, possibly thirty thousand years ago. They must have travelled down through the East Indies and crossed over to Australia by boats or rafts, bringing their dogs with them. The mammals living there, kangaroos, koala bears and duck-billed platypuses were unlike those in the rest of the world. Man and the dog were the first modern mammals to break into Australia, some thousands of years ago, and were rediscovered as the Aborigine and the dingo by European explorers in the seventeenth century.

The first arrival of man in America was also in the Pleistocene era, probably about twenty-five thousand years ago, (although one recent estimate puts it several thousand years earlier). American Indians have Mongolian facial features and it seems certain that they crossed from Siberia into Alaska via what is now the Bering Strait. At that time the world was in the middle of an ice age, with thick glaciers cover-

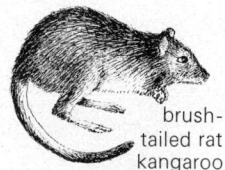

brush-tailed rat kangaroo

koala

wombat

dingo

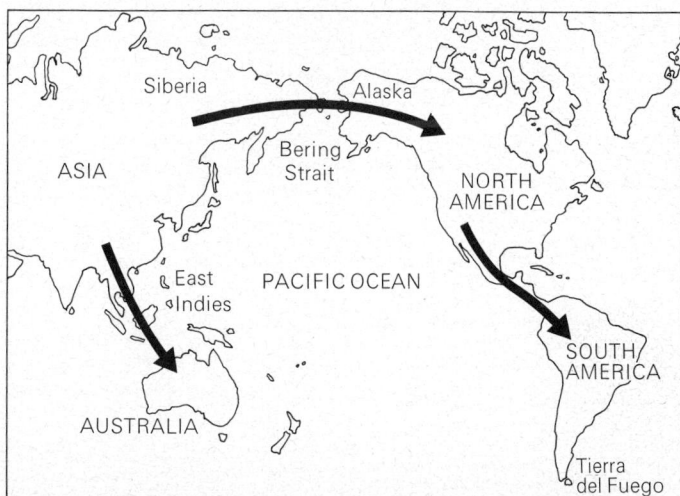

ing vast areas of the North American continent. So much water was frozen that the level of the sea was lowered, and a broad land-bridge connected Asia to America, allowing men and animals to wander into the New World. The Indians must have spread very quickly because bones of extinct animals, scored by stone tools and possibly fourteen thousand years old, have been found at Lake Maracaibo in Venezuela. In Tierra del Fuego, near the southern tip of South America, well-made stone tools dating from eleven thousand years ago have also been unearthed in caves. The Indians needed to adapt their way of life considerably as they gradually moved into the very different habitats throughout the continent, ranging from the frozen tundra of northern Canada to the tropical forests of Brazil. The spread was probably forced on them by population growth and the resulting lack of land for hunting or farming. It may well have taken a thousand years to travel each thousand miles down the length of the continent. However, during this period of expansion, differences in dress, language, religion and custom all had time to develop between the tribes.

The colonization of the Pacific Islands probably took place after the Pleistocene era. Many anthropologists think the islanders came directly from Asia, but another opinion is that Indians may have drifted along ocean currents on rafts from the west coast of South America until they reached the South Sea Islands. Thor Heyerdahl tested this hypothesis dramatically by drifting to Polynesia from South America on his balsa-wood raft *Kon Tiki*.

Modern migrations

The migrations of early man probably took place because territories were overcrowded or food was short. Modern population movements do not depend so directly on these biological factors. Technology insulates people from direct biological pressures, and migrations are now more likely to be the result of political or cultural factors. Even so, there are always biological limits to man's environment. For example, even with the help of modern technology we cannot live contentedly for very long where the temperature is too hot or too cold, or where there is no soil to grow food.

By far the biggest migration in man's history was the exodus from Europe during the nineteenth century. Probably as many as seventy million people left to settle chiefly in America, Australia and South Africa. The early migrants to North America were mainly from the countries on the Atlantic coast of Europe, but as communications and information improved, more people came from Eastern and Southern Europe, bringing the total number of immigrants to the United States and Canada to about forty-five million. Approximately twenty million people settled in South and Central America, coming chiefly from Spain, Portugal and Italy, and about five million travelled to Australia, New Zealand and South Africa.

Before the nineteenth century, the people who emigrated were often adventurers, deported criminals or political and religious refugees. There are several reasons for the massive emigration in the nineteenth century. The continent of Europe was unsettled after the Napoleonic wars, land was scarce due to population growth, the development of machine industries produced a depression of wages and increased unemployment, and transport was much improved. Everyone expected a higher standard of living in the country to which they emigrated.

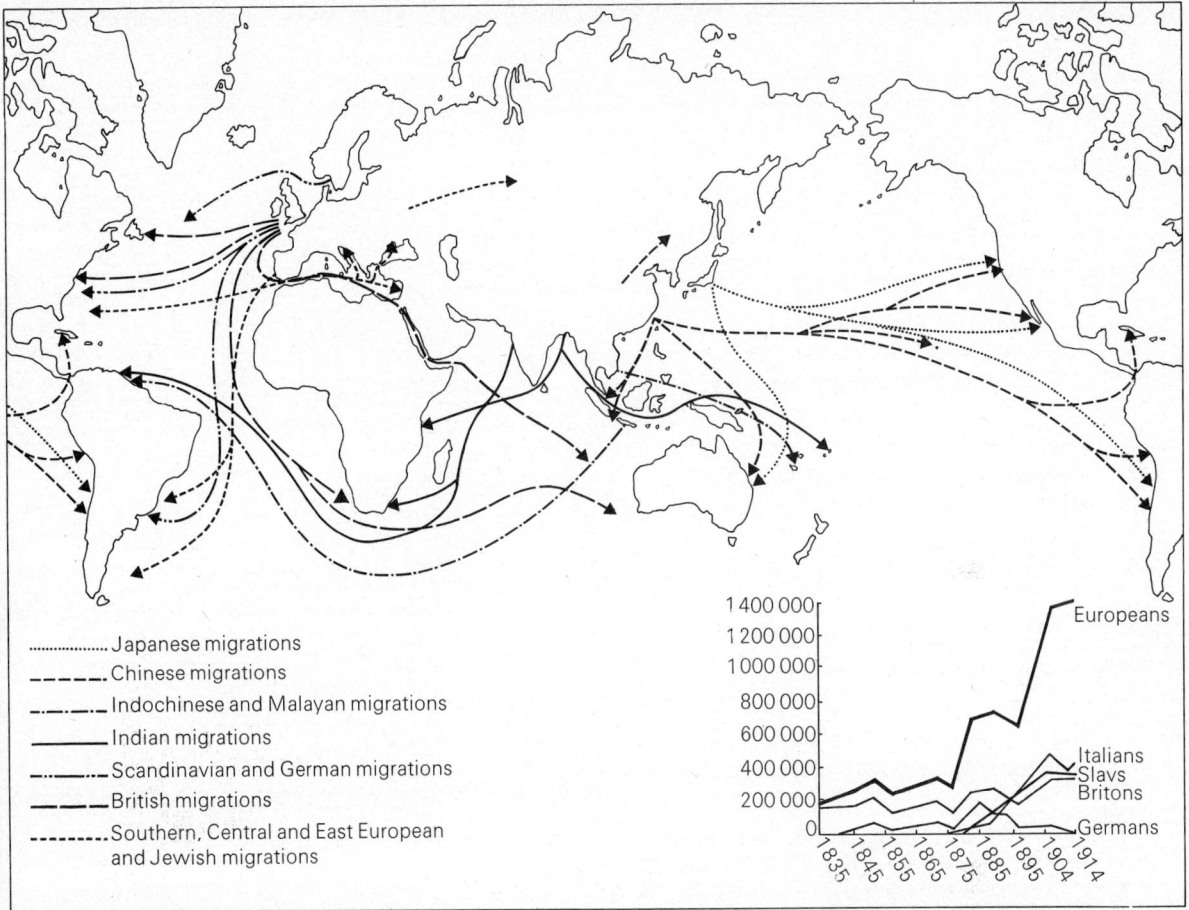

.... Japanese migrations

– – – – –. Chinese migrations

–..–..–. Indochinese and Malayan migrations

————— Indian migrations

–.—.—.—.Scandinavian and German migrations

– — – — British migrations

– – – – – –Southern, Central and East European
and Jewish migrations

Some of the great migrations that have taken place.
The inset shows how many Europeans were involved.

Population statistics show that the volume of migration alters as economic conditions alter. Emigration to the United States has increased in times of economic prosperity and decreased in times of slump, and following the First World War there was a large increase in immigrants from Europe. Because North America is relatively close to Europe, and has vast natural resources, approximately 60 per cent of all European emigrants chose to settle there. South America also has great natural resources, but there are geographic and climatic obstacles to settlement in large parts of the interior, and so far fewer people have made their homes there.

Caged prisoners on a transport ship bound for Botany Bay, Australia.

Thor Heyerdahl

Thor Heyerdahl is a Norwegian scientist who has been very interested in the Polynesian culture and in theories about where the people in South America came from. He organized a number of expeditions which were designed to prove the experts wrong. In 1947 he undertook the *Kon-Tiki* expedition from Peru across the Pacific to the Polynesian Islands. In 1969, he set out in a papyrus boat, Ra, from Morocco to test the theory that the ancient Egyptians could have crossed the Atlantic and set up communities in Mexico, Peru and Chile.

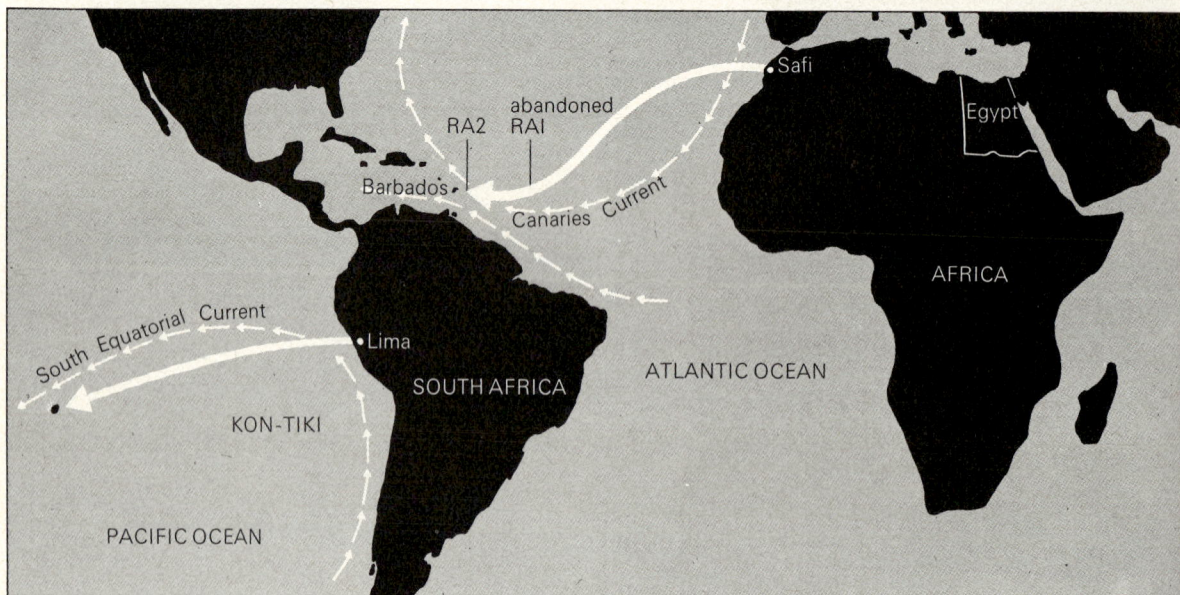

Safi

Egypt

RA2

abandoned
RAI

Barbados

Canaries Current

AFRICA

South Equatorial Current

Lima

SOUTH AFRICA

ATLANTIC OCEAN

KON-TIKI

PACIFIC OCEAN

Kon-Tiki

'An ordinary day on board the *Kon-Tiki* began with the last night-watch shaking some life into the cook, who crawled out sleepily onto the dewy deck in the morning sun and began to gather flying fish. Instead of eating the fish raw, according to both Polynesian and Peruvian recipes, we fried them over a small primus stove at the bottom of a box which stood lashed fast to the deck outside the cabin door. This box was our kitchen. Here there was usually shelter from the South-East trade wind which regularly blew onto our other quarter. Only when wind and sea juggled too much with the primus flame did this set fire to the wooden box, and once, when the cook had fallen asleep, the whole box became a mass of flames which spread to the very wall of the bamboo cabin. But the fire on the wall was quickly put out when the smoke poured into the hut, for, after all, we had never far to go for water on board the *Kon-Tiki*.'

Then at the end of the voyage,

'The *Kon-Tiki* still lay far out on the reef with the spray flying over her. She was a wreck, but an honourable wreck. Everything above deck was smashed up, but the nine balsa logs from the Quivedo forest in Ecuador were as intact as ever. They had saved our lives. The sea had claimed but little of the cargo, and none of what we had stowed inside the cabin.'

Ra

Thor Heyerdahl explained what he was trying to do when he set out on the expedition.

'I wanted to find out if a boat like this could be used at sea. I wanted to find out if it was true, as the experts believed, that the Phoenicians had to come to the Nile to gather the papyrus, because the Egyptians themselves were unable to sail their reed boats outside the Nile Delta. I wanted to find out if the ancient Egyptians themselves had originally been seafarers, before they settled down to become sculptors, pharaohs and mummies. I wanted to find out if a reed boat could withstand a sea voyage of 250 miles, the distance from Egypt to Lebanon. I wanted to find out if a reed boat would be able to sail still further, even from one continent to another. I wanted to find out if a reed boat could make the journey to America.'

Internal migrations

People are much more likely to migrate fairly short distances inside their own countries than they are to make long journeys half way across the world. In several countries there is a well-established trend in population movements. Thus, in Great Britain the population tends to move towards the south-east corner of the country, in Germany the trend is from east to west, in Italy from south to north and in the United States from east to west. In each of these cases people move towards a richer part of the country. However, the shift in the Soviet Union, which is from European to Asiatic Russia, is much more like the pushing back of the Western Frontier which took place in the nineteenth century in the United States, and has been encouraged by the Soviet Government.

Birmingham

London

large increase

small increase

decrease

There has been a general movement of the population towards south-east England in recent years. At the same time people have been moving out of the large city centres. The preliminary results of the 1971 census show that both these trends are continuing.

Apart from movements of the type mentioned, one thing which is happening in all industrial countries is the shift from the country into the town. In general, the larger the city, the more attractive it is to immigrants. Also, the more technically advanced a nation is, the more quickly the population is drawn into the towns.

Factors affecting population distribution

In spite of ease of travel, most of the Earth's land surface today is still uninhabited, and there are also large areas occupied by few and widely separated communities. There are four major areas with dense populations: the Far East, India, Europe and eastern North America. There are also several smaller centres of population, including Java, south-east Australia, the Nile Floodplain, the Guinea Coast of Africa, south-eastern South America and the Pacific coast of North America. We might expect population movements to be from regions of dense to regions of sparse population, but this is not always true. For example, the Nile Valley has been thickly populated for several thousand years and yet there is little evidence of people leaving the valley to live in the surrounding region. It is better to think in terms of movements from areas of poor economic prospects to those where economic possibilities are higher. But these depend upon biological and geographical considerations.

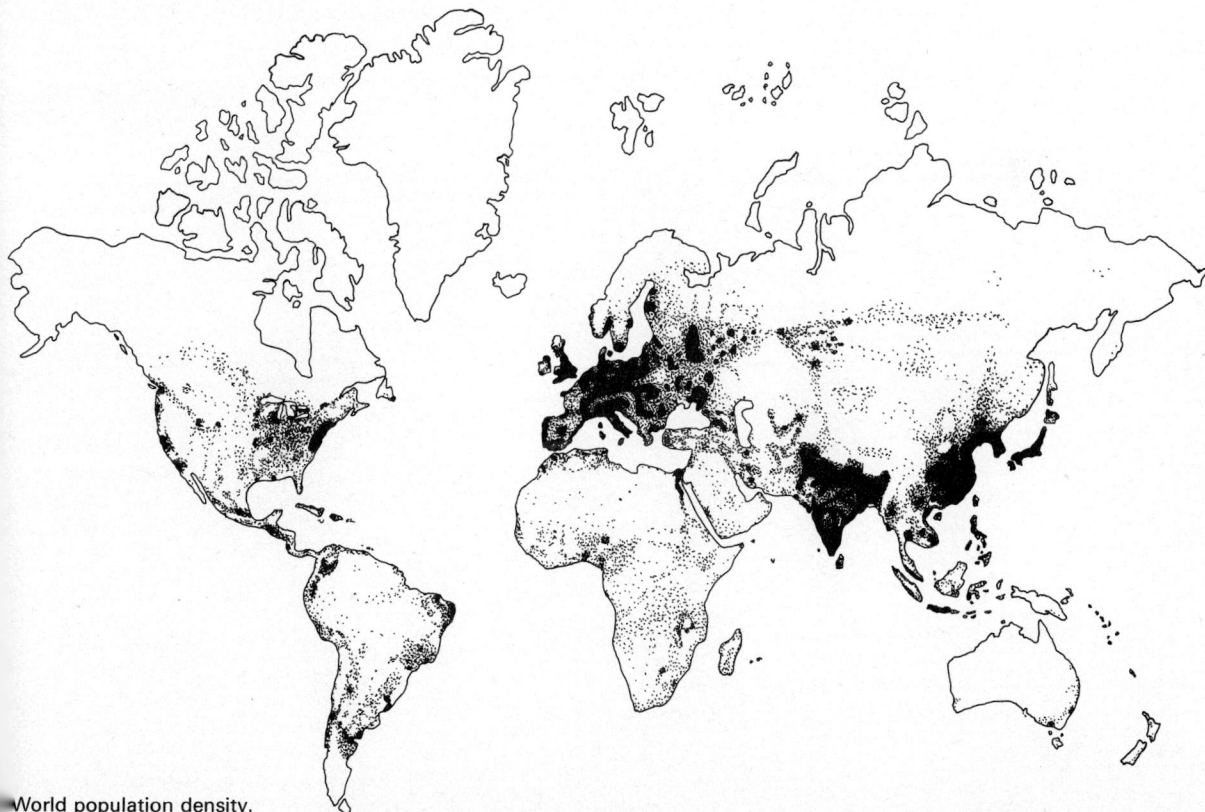

World population density.

Climate

Man does not like cold climates. Polar and sub-polar regions have the lowest human population densities of all. In these areas people are very likely to catch respiratory diseases. Also the shortness of the growing season cuts down the amount of food which can be produced, and it may be that the long periods of darkness and lack of sunlight have other physical and psychological ill-effects on man, about which we do not yet know much.

High temperatures, when combined with high humidity, allow plants to grow very rapidly so that more than one crop can be harvested per year. The warmth also cuts down the need for food and shelter, so that high densities of people are possible in tropical and subtropical countries. However, in these warmer climates, insects, fungi and bacteria can reproduce in large numbers so that there is an increased chance of the spread of disease in man, crops and domestic animals. In colder regions the winter serves as an annual check on reproduction, but there is no such seasonal control in the tropics.

When high temperatures are combined with low rainfall, soil moisture can fall to such a low level that plants are virtually unable to grow. Desert lands take up about 18 per cent of the Earth's land surface and contain only about 4 per cent of its population. Population centres which do exist in desert regions are commonly associated with water supplies coming from outside. The Lower Nile Valley is an example of this type of centre.

Landform

Landform is another major factor affecting population distribution. People tend to con-

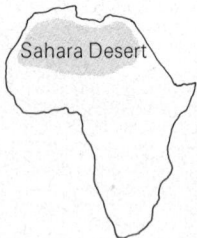

Sahara Desert

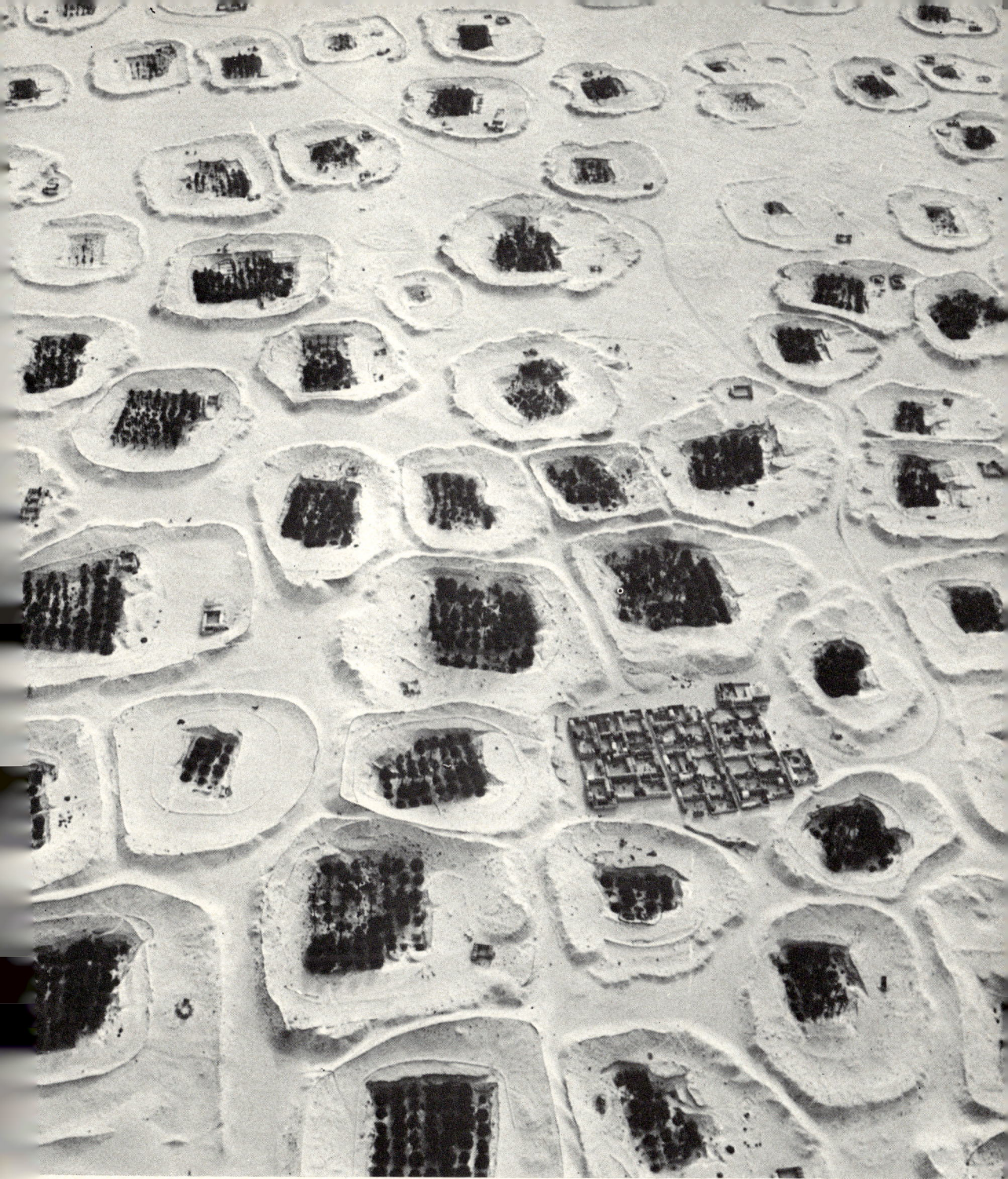

Each of these 'pancakes' in the Sahara desert is a tiny man-made oasis of palm trees. Underground water is tapped for the trees which are planted in hollows 6–12 metres deep, surrounded by fencing to stop the trees being covered by blowing sand.

Tristan da Cunha

The only habitable land on Tristan da Cunha is a narrow strip between the mountains and the sea. The island is volcanic and the island was evacuated when it erupted. When the danger was over, many of the islanders chose to return.

centrate where the shape of the land is hospitable. Mountainous country is difficult to live in because of the shortage of land which can be farmed. Also, the oxygen in the highlands is less dense and makes breathing less efficient. Another difficulty is that it is very expensive to transport through mountainous country the machinery and materials necessary for technological development. In fact nine-tenths of mankind lives below a height of four hundred metres above sea level and, in general, population density goes down as the height of the land goes up. Because life in the plains is relatively easy there is a tendency for slow and continuous migration out of mountainous areas. Thus, the highland areas of Britain are severely depopulated because of the movement of the young people to the lowlands. Lowland soils are often more fertile and, especially in regions of grassland and broad-leaved forests where the soil is very rich, tend to attract dense populations.

Social and economic influence

As a society becomes more complex, biological factors become less important in controlling its distribution. Technological developments have increased the temperature range within which people can live and work, and the distance at which they can live from the sources of food supply. Millions of people may live in cities and obtain their food from hundreds or even thousands of miles away.

Social and economic factors also influence the distribution of population. Let us look at two examples. Firstly, cultural similarities usually determine the country to which people will emigrate. People leaving Britain usually settle in countries where English is the national language, Spaniards and Portuguese tend to go to South America, and so on. Secondly, people tend to migrate to the sites of industrial raw materials such as coal and iron; or to places along communication routes, such as New York, which acts as a gateway to the interior of the United States.

Broadly speaking then, even in industrial society biological factors control to some extent the migration of people, although other factors become equally if not more important. In one respect human beings behave in a similar way to the rest of the animal world. Migrants come mostly from the young mature section of the population, rather than from the older, more firmly established adults. But today, the increase in birth-rates and the decline in death-rates have been far more important in determining population density in any one area, than has migration.

Life at high altitudes

'The Quechua Indians inhabit the lofty plateaux of Peru; and Alcide d'Orbigny states that, from continually breathing a highly rarified atmosphere, they have acquired chests and lungs of extraordinary dimensions. The cells, also, of the lungs are larger and more numerous than in Europeans. These observations have been doubted; but Mr D. Forbes carefully measured many Aymaras, an allied race, living at the height of between 10 000 and 15 000 feet; and he informs me that they differ conspicuously from the men of all other races seen by him in the circumference and length of their bodies. In his table of measurements the stature of each man is taken at 1000, and the other measurements are reduced to this standard. It is here seen that the extended arms of the Aymaras are shorter than those of Europeans, and much shorter than those of Negroes. The legs are likewise shorter; and they present this remarkable peculiarity that in every Aymara measured the femur is actually shorter than the tibia. On an average, the length of the femur to that of the tibia is as 211 to 252; whilst in two Europeans, measured at the same time, the femora to the tibiae were as 244 to 230; and in three Negroes as 258 to 241. The humerus is likewise shorter relatively to the forearm. This shortening of that part of the limb which is nearest to the body, appears to be, as suggested to me by Mr Forbes, a case of compensation in relation with the greatly increased length of the trunk. The Aymaras present some other singular points of structure, for instance, the very small projection of the heel.'

from *The Descent of Man*,
Charles Darwin

A deserted village
high in the Andes.

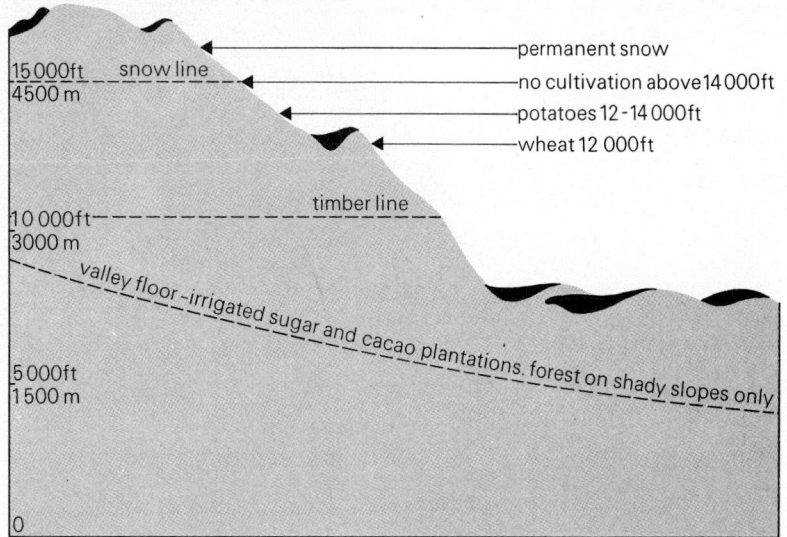

15 000 ft
4500 m — snow line

permanent snow
no cultivation above 14 000 ft
potatoes 12 - 14 000 ft
wheat 12 000 ft

timber line

10 000 ft
3000 m

valley floor - irrigated sugar and cacao plantations. forest on shady slopes only

5 000 ft
1500 m

0

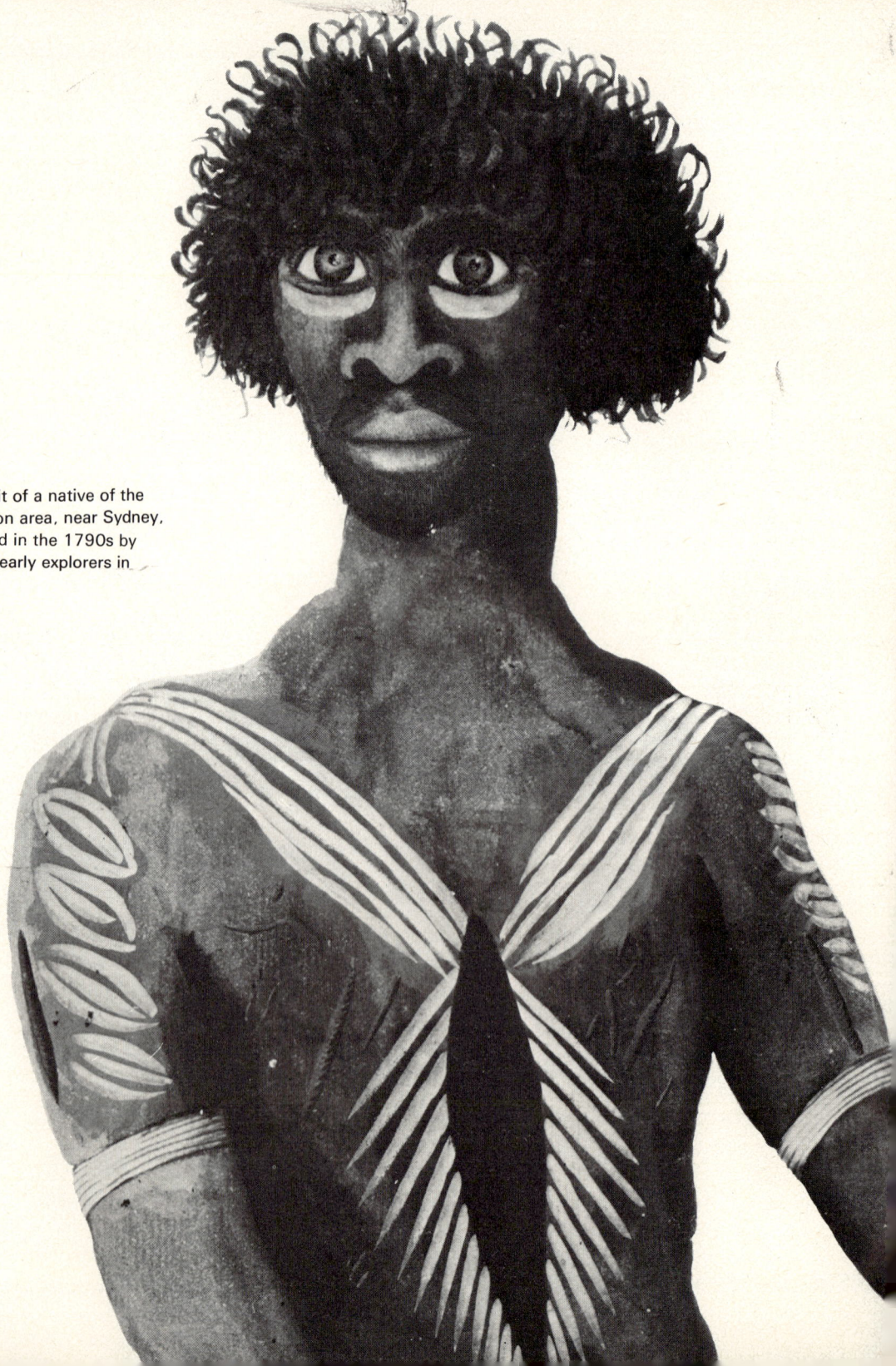

This portrait of a native of the
Port Jackson area, near Sydney,
was painted in the 1790s by
one of the early explorers in
Australia.

5 Traditional peoples

Perhaps man is not a suitable subject for studies of population ecology, because cultural and technical developments have been so great that he is cut off from the effects of his natural environment. However, we have seen that this is not completely true even for people in very complex societies. In simple human societies, biological factors have a surprisingly large influence on population size.

For example, it is possible to work out the biological 'success' of an animal by comparing the amount of food eaten by a population with the amount of all sorts of food actually available. In 1948, O. P. Pearson collected figures for the north-eastern United States which compared the success of the local Indian tribes and that of the other animals in the area. It turned out that the Indians had rather less impact on the available food supply than deer, and about the same impact as the local population of long-tailed shrews. In fact the culture of the Indians affects the way they use their environment; for example, it determines whether it is acceptable for people to eat this or that animal or plant.

Even at the animal level, population density can be affected by behaviour which is learnt rather than inbuilt. An experiment with rats where too much food was always available showed that the population density also depended on the fact that young rats learned how to defend an area of territory, and would not allow outsiders to enter it.

Australian tribesmen

Australia is the only place where a whole continent of people whose life was based on hunting and collecting food survived to modern times. The Aborigines live the kind of life which was universal in the Old Stone Age. Like all human groups, the Aborigines have a population structure and density which is controlled partly by environment and partly by custom. The basic unit is the family, which is like any family, consisting of an adult man with one or more women and their children. In addition to the family there are two larger social groups, the horde and the tribe. A horde is made up of a man and his wife or wives, their children and their respective husbands or wives. This collection of grandparents, aunts, uncles, cousins and so on, in the West, is sometimes called the extended family. It usually numbers about forty people and is the main land-owning unit. Members of the horde are not allowed to marry each other and when a male chooses a wife from outside, she comes to live in the territory of the horde. The tribe consists of a group of hordes united by a common dialect (and this presumably means a common line of descent), and by a common set of customs; but there is no one in authority formally binding the hordes into a tribal unit. Most tribes have between two hundred and nine hundred members, and the typical size is five hundred. There is very little marriage between members of different tribes.

Families are the basic unit of this society. In those parts of Australia where there is an arid season with food shortage, the horde breaks up into individual families. Not only do the families require less food than the horde but, because the horde is split up, food gathering can be more efficient within the territory. Migration to new territory often occurs because there is a food shortage and it seems likely that the family is the migratory unit among the Aborigines, although, apparently, once a new territory has been colonized, the occupying family often persuades the rest of the horde to join it.

Population and rainfall

There are about six hundred tribes in Australia and when the first Europeans arrived the population was probably about three hundred thousand. J. B. Birdsell, an American anthropologist, wanted to find out if there was a connection between territory size and rainfall. He chose 123 tribes which were similar in the following ways: (a) on average there were about five hundred people in each tribe, (b) the water in their territories came from rainfall and not from rivers flowing into the area and (c) they obtained all their food from the land and not from the sea or from rivers. By excluding regions which did not fit these conditions, he obtained a group of tribes of approximately the same size, living in the same sort of environment, apart from differences in rainfall which ranged from 5 to 151 inches per year. For each of the tribes he compared the amount of rain falling with the size of the area occupied by the tribe.

Nonnia

A. F. Cudmore in 1893 wrote in the *Journal of the Australian Association for the Advancement of Science* an account of one forced family migration:

'It appears that, about thirty years ago, "Nonnia" (who is now about sixty years of age), for some reason not rightly known, bolted from Popiltah Lake with one or two Lubras (women) and hid himself in the dense tract of mallee which covers the country for about six hundred square miles along the South Australian and New South Wales boundary, from about the thirtieth to the eighty-first mile post. Here he had carefully concealed himself from the whites and blacks, living on kangaroo and whatever else he could get hold of, and obtained water from the roots of the red mallee and the needle or water-bush.

'During this thirty years the old gentleman has raised quite a little family around him and is now the proud father and grandfather of about twenty-eight men, women and children, over all of whom he reigns supreme and his word is law.'

In 1940 the descendents of Nonnia were identified as the Nanja horde of the Maraura tribe. Most Australian women become mothers for the first time around the age of sixteen. If this were the interval between generations in the case of Nonnia's family, then by the time Cudmore was writing, about two generations would have passed since Nonnia bolted from the lake. With a population at that time of twenty-eight, there must have been at least a trebling of numbers at each generation in a tract of land without surface water and with very little animal and plant life.

Mallee gums and spinifex grass in South Australia.

Birdsell found that from his results he could draw a graph relating the size of the tribal territory to the amount of rainfall and expressed the relationship by the equation

$$y = 7112 \cdot 8x^{-1 \cdot 5845},$$

where y is the size of the tribal territory and x is the mean annual rainfall. The equation was sufficiently accurate to give him an 80 per cent chance of correctly predicting the size of a tribal territory from a knowledge of the rainfall. Biologists studying the ecology of other mammals have also generally found that the density of the population of the given species is related to some variable in the environment, such as rainfall or temperature.

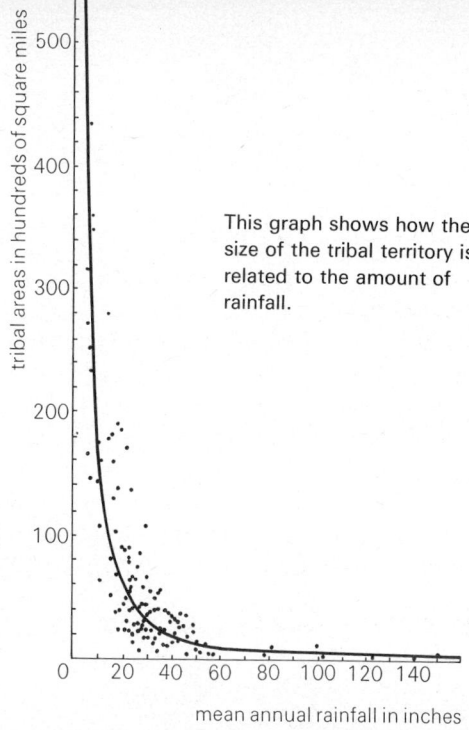

This graph shows how the size of the tribal territory is related to the amount of rainfall.

mean annual rainfall in inches

A whole series of initiation ceremonies, such as this ordeal by fire, have to be undergone before a man can become a full adult member of the Arunta, an Aborigine tribe of Australia.

The first important thing to note is that, in a dry climate, rainfall, or the lack of it, limits the density of plant life which can grow in an area. Man stands at the head of several food chains, exploiting all the lower animal and plant levels, so he in turn responds sensitively to differences in rainfall. Birdsell lists the diet of tribesmen living along the south-western coastal regions of Western Australia to show how completely Aborigines exploit the food available.

Some of the many plants and animals which Aborigines will eat.

Animal foods (figures indicate the number of kinds of each available)

marsupials smaller than rabbits : 5

marsupial rats and mice : 9

opossums : 2

dingoes : 1

kangaroos : 6

all birds, including emus and turkeys

iguanas and lizards : 7

snakes : 8

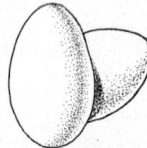
eggs of every species of bird and lizard

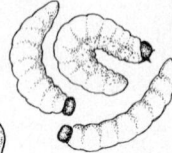
grubs : 4

frogs : 11

whales

turtles : 3

seals : 2

fish : 29

freshwater shellfish : 4

all saltwater shellfish except oysters

seeds of several species of pea-type plants

Plant foods

roots : 29

fruit : 4

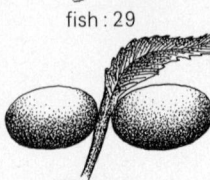
cycad nuts : 4

other nuts : 2

mesembryanthemum (a composite flower) : 2

fungus : 7

gum : 4

manna : 2

flowers of several species of Banksia

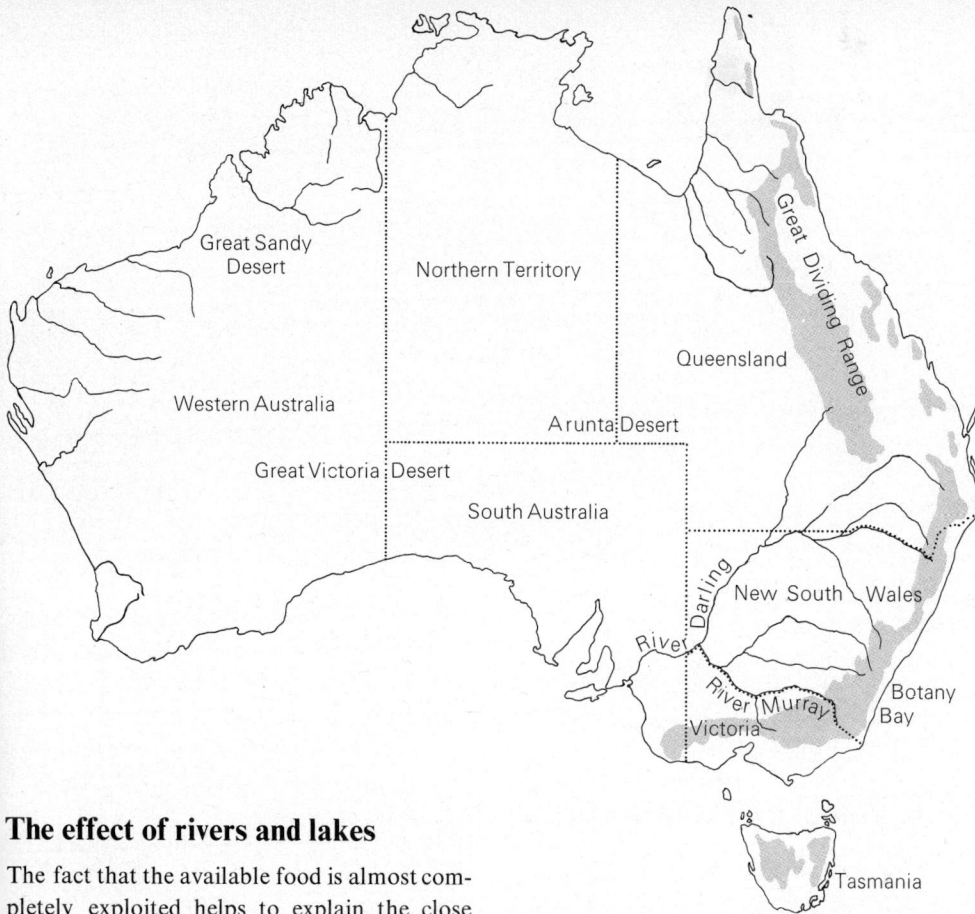

Great Sandy Desert

Northern Territory

Queensland

Great Dividing Range

Western Australia

Arunta Desert

Great Victoria Desert

South Australia

River Darling

New South Wales

River Murray

Victoria

Botany Bay

Tasmania

The effect of rivers and lakes

The fact that the available food is almost completely exploited helps to explain the close relationship between rainfall and the numbers of people in an area. What is the effect of having another source of water available apart from rainfall? Among the tribes excluded from the one hundred and twenty-three chosen by Birdsell, were some who lived in areas containing 'unearned surface water'. This means that a river or lake inside the territory depends for its existence on rainfall in distant regions. The Murray and Darling Rivers have their sources on the western slopes of the Dividing Range and flow through country which becomes more and more arid until along much of their course they pass through land which has only fifteen to twenty inches of rainfall per year. For the people living near the banks of the river the water provides an 'unearned' resource. The effect of this is that the nine tribes occupying the lowest part of the Murray River have a population density between seventeen and thirty-three times greater than that expected from a knowledge of the rainfall. Lake Alexandrina, at the mouth of the Murray River, is well supplied with animal and plant life, and the five tribes living near the lake have a population almost forty times greater than expected.

The nearness of the sea also has an effect on population density. Tribes living on islands in the sea have higher densities than could be predicted from rainfall, and for many tribes living on the coast of the mainland the density is intermediate between that found on the islands and densities inland.

Other traditional peoples

Among the tribes that Birdsell studied there seemed to be a strict relationship between population density and rainfall. The population density of any traditional tribe living in an area where there is not much rain might depend upon the rainfall in the same way, but of course there are other possibilities. Eskimos living in the Arctic would show densities conditioned by the temperature and the length of the growing season, because these are the factors which are most important for the growth of plant and animal life in the polar regions.

Sometimes, regions which appear similar do not have the same population densities. Bushmen in the African Kalahari Desert live in denser populations than Australians, and the Baja Indians of the southern Californian Desert have an average population density fifty times that of the Australian Aborigines. Although in many detailed ways the cultures of the three groups differ, they all obtain their food by very simple methods such as digging with bare hands or with a digging stick, or by hunting with a spear or bow and arrow. What matters much more is that there are large differences in the

Kalahari Desert

Canada

Both Eskimos and Bushmen are totally dependent on their surroundings for food, water and shelter. The Bushmen who live in the Kalahari desert of south-west Africa, are filling ostrich eggshells with water sucked from an underground spring. The Eskimos are patiently waiting by a blow hole in the ice for a seal to come up for air.

food chains in the three regions. Bushmen, for example, can depend on larger supplies of grazing animals than Australians, and Baja Indians have far better supplies of starchy foods.

However, when people reach the agricultural stage they are to some extent altering the environment to suit themselves, and therefore becoming less dependent on the 'given' habitat. In an industrial civilization, the alterations which man can make to his surroundings are so vast that it is meaningless to talk about population control in simple biological terms. But even here, the limits against which technologists must strive to make the deserts or the ice fields of the world inhabitable by modern man are all biological.

The extreme example of this is the ingenious ways in which space biologists maintain the temperature, pressure and humidity in spacecraft so that men can live comfortably. They have had to provide continuous supplies of oxygen, water and food. They also had to devise methods of recycling carbon dioxide and urine so that they can help to provide more oxygen and water respectively, to meet the basic biological demands of the human body.

6 Modern population growth

Bacteria reproduce by splitting in half every twenty minutes. If there was nothing to stop their growth, after thirty-six hours a layer of bacteria a foot deep would cover the entire surface of the Earth. This has not happened, so there must be natural checks to free growth; exactly the same must be true of all living things, including man.

The maximum population

People often say that Malthus's 'dismal theorem' has been proved wrong because the world population continues to increase at a very rapid rate and, at the same time, the standard of living, of Europeans at least, has been greatly improved. But in fact most people in the world still do not get enough to eat. This is not so much due to a world lack of food as to political difficulties and ignorance. In 1964 the United States Government rented twenty million acres from farmers to stop them growing too much food. One study suggested that another sixty-two and a half million acres ought to be withdrawn from American farmland to prevent a surplus in relation to the market. If there is a surplus, the price of food drops to such a low level that the farmer cannot make a living from selling his crops. Similar situations exist in, for example, Australia, Canada and New Zealand.

About 11 per cent of the total land area of the world is cultivated, and eventually more than 55 per cent might be made arable. This view, which is considered over-optimistic by many scientists, is held by Colin Clark. He calculates that, if this area were farmed with the efficiency of Dutch farmers, it would support a population of about twenty-eight thousand million people, or at Japanese levels of farming and nutrition, a total of ninety-five thousand million. At the moment there are between three and four thousand million people in the world; if growth-rates do not slow down there will be twenty-eight thousand million people in about a hundred years' time.

Thomas Malthus

In the eighteenth century the Reverend Thomas Malthus noted that human populations could double each generation. This had happened in the colonies in the new and almost empty North American continent. But in Europe, the population growth-rate was much lower and he believed this was related to the fact that food production could not be increased at nearly such a fast rate in the old countries of Europe, as was possible in theory for the human population.

An unchecked population can double at least every twenty-five years, increasing in the ratio of one, two, four, eight, sixteen, thirty-two, etc. But the development of new land in Europe could only possibly increase by the same amount every generation, in the ratio of one, two, three, four, five, six and so on. So if initially there was enough food for the population, and the normal increase occurred, within 225 years the ratio of population to the amount of food available would be 512:10. Malthus graphically describes the processes preventing population running ahead of food supply:

'The power of population is so superior to the power in the earth to produce subsistence for man, that premature death must in some shape or other visit the human race. The vices of mankind are active and able ministers of depopulation. They are the precursors in the great army of destruction; and often finish the dreadful work themselves. But should they fail in this war of extermination, sickly seasons, epidemics, pestilence and plague advance in terrifying array and sweep off their thousands and ten thousands. Should success be still incomplete, gigantic inevitable famine stalks in the rear, and with one mighty blow, levels the population with the food of the world.'

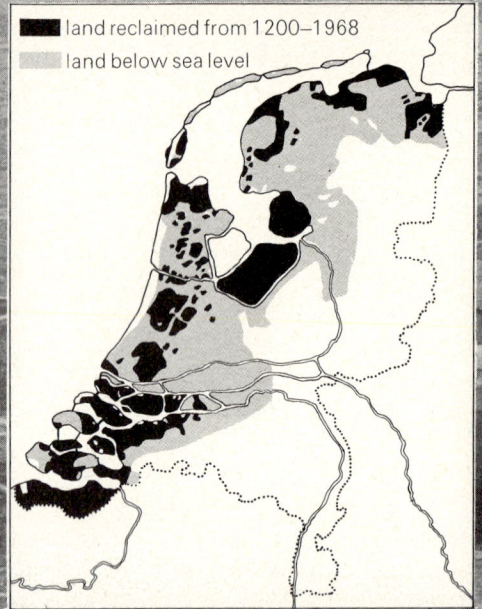

land reclaimed from 1200–1968
land below sea level

The Dutch have been reclaiming land from the sea since the year 1200. Much of Holland now stands below sea level with huge dykes keeping the sea out. These two aerial photographs show how a scheme to recover land from the sea has transformed an island into a piece of the mainland.

J. H. Fremlin recently tried to work out the theoretical limit to the human population. He calculated the absolute maximum to be sixty thousand million million people, which would be reached, at present rates of growth, in eight hundred and ninety years' time. By this time, all other living creatures would have been wiped out to make room for man and his 'servicing' machinery. The polar ice-caps would have melted and the whole Earth would have an equatorial climate, due to the thousands of orbiting mirrors which would be used to reflect extra solar energy onto the Earth for photosynthesis. About six or seven hundred years from now, however, photosynthesis would not be able to provide enough food for the thousand million million population. From then on, food would have to be synthesized chemically and waste products and dead bodies would also have to be reprocessed for food. The true limiting factor would not be shortage of food, but the overheating of the Earth. At the final population

A model city of the future. Will we have the space and resources to build like this?

density of one hundred and twenty people per square metre, all free atmosphere would have to be removed from the surface of the Earth to allow excess heat to radiate directly and quickly into outer space. Even so, the outer-skin temperature of the Earth would be about 2000°C, and Fremlin does not see how the human population could develop refrigeration machinery to deal with any further temperature increases.

He does not consider emigration to other planets as a possible solution, since to keep the world population at its present size we ought to be sending out seventy million people per year *now*. Housing one hundred and twenty people per square metre presents some problems. These would have to be met by building a continuous two-thousand-storey building to cover the entire land and sea surface of the Earth. This would provide each person with seven and a half square metres of floor space in one thousand storeys, and leaves the other thousand for food production and refrigeration machinery. People would be confined to a personal cubicle with liquid food pumped in and wastes pumped out. Would life be worth living under these circumstances?

Overpopulation

If providing enough food is not an insoluble problem then what do we mean by overpopulation? There are many aspects of life which become more difficult and unpleasant as the population increases. When this becomes a really serious problem, we can speak of overpopulation. There are several ways of looking at this.

In developing countries

Can the world feed its people? It is possible; but will it happen during the next twenty years, taking into account the speed of population growth and the economically backward position of many countries where the population is increasing most rapidly? The difference between industrialized countries and developing countries in the amount of food available is getting greater.

In the 1930s, Africa, Asia and Latin America were actually exporting about twelve million tons of surplus grain. In 1960, this surplus had disappeared, and Asia and Africa between them had to import eighteen million tons of grain. Between 1956 and 1966, 2 per cent less food was grown in the developing countries of the world, while their populations increased by about forty-five million. In India, although agricultural productivity increased by 1·6 per cent in 1968, the population increased by 2·7 per cent. Populations are increasing but food production is not keeping pace or is often actually decreasing.

The solution to the problem is not simply a matter of working out how to reduce population growth. Pakistan, which has a similar population growth-rate to India increased its agricultural productivity by 5 per cent in 1968 and, had it not been for the disasters in Bangladesh, would by 1971 have been able to provide enough food for itself. The heartbreaking race to feed the world population is failing, not only because of rapid population growth, but because so many countries have backward agriculture, low industrial activity (or the reverse, over-insistence on early expansion of heavy industry), inadequate markets, international monetary policies dictated by the rich nations, political corruption, apathy and fatalism, and poor education. While population-control measures must be taken quickly to bring down the birth-rate, they must be combined with carefully planned agricultural and educational development.

'Ask them to move back —
and hurry!'

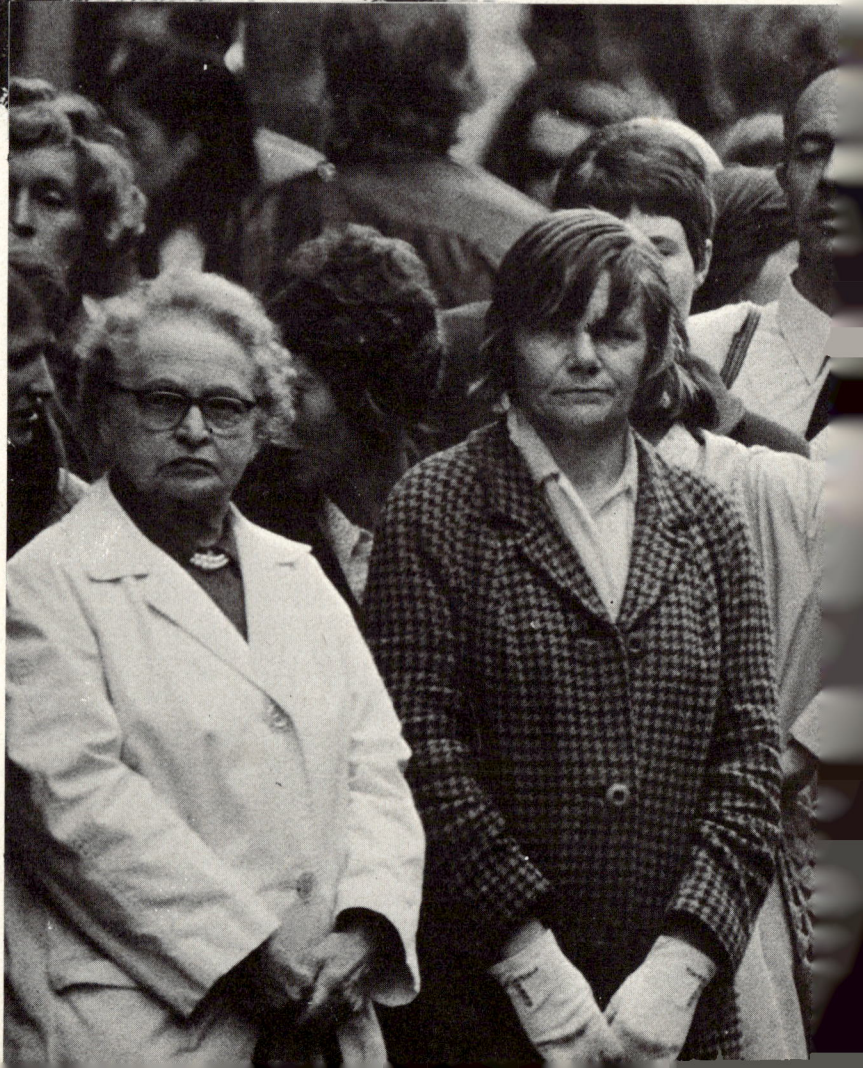

Faces show the stress of
living in overcrowded cities.

Overcrowding

When certain animals live in densely crowded conditions, their behaviour becomes abnormal. Studies on the snowshoe hare, mentioned in chapter 1 as an example of an animal with a cyclical population growth, showed that when the animals were dying off in large numbers there was usually plenty of food. They had not starved to death. When the corpses were studied it was found that the liver had shrunk and contained lower amounts of glycogen than normal, the blood-sugar level was below normal and there were haemorrhages in the brain, adrenal glands, thyroid gland and kidneys. It was also noticed that before they died the hares usually went into convulsions.

All these symptoms are typical of an animal which has suffered severe stress. Experiments have shown that in a stressed animal the pituitary and adrenal glands are overactive. These glands help animals adapt to a new situation. Excess secretions are triggered off whenever

anything seems to threaten the animal. There are three stages in the response to stress: (a) alarm, where the animal tries to adapt to the new situation, (b) resistence, when adaptation is at a maximum and (c) exhaustion, when adaptation fails. When prolonged stress results in exhaustion, anxiety and severe changes in behaviour occur in man and other animals. High blood pressure, stomach ulcers, skin disorders and asthma may all be the result of stress.

In the case of the snowshoe hare, the stress seems to have been due to overcrowding. There are many cases of stress, apparently due to overcrowding, recorded for other animals, such as rodents (various species), deer and animals in zoos.

One of the best known of these studies is the research of John Calhoun on crowding in the wild Norway rat. He kept rats in a quarter-acre enclosure with plenty of food and water. After twenty-seven months the population had stabilized itself at one hundred and fifty adults, even though the expected population by this time should have been five thousand. In further experiments Calhoun began to find out what had been happening. Not only did many new-born rats die, but as the density increased many pregnancies were aborted and many mothers died. Often the mothers could not feed their young or make nests. The males showed various forms of abnormal behaviour including homosexuality, cannibalism, frenzied over-activity and, in some cases, pathological withdrawal so that they came out of their nests only to eat and drink. These breakdowns in social behaviour happened at a population density only twice that which had been found acceptable to the rats from the point of view of stress.

Population density may also be important for man. Desmond Morris thinks that the stress experienced by modern city dwellers is related to man's social origin as a tribal animal living in groups of much the same size as the Australian Aboriginal 'horde'. Stress diseases are common amongst city dwellers, as are crimes of violence. In the wild, animals do not usually develop stomach ulcers, or kill and maim other members of their own species, but this does happen when they are packed densely together in cages in zoos. Morris talks of the city as the 'human zoo'. People tolerate city life because they expect to make more money there and also because, although it is stressful, it is also exciting. Morris believes that unless there is careful replanning of cities combined with a check on the growth of the population, there is a danger that the human zoo will 'proliferate into a gigantic lunatic asylum, like one of the hideously cramped animal menageries of the last century'.

Pollution

As population growth speeds up, more food, machinery and energy resources are needed, and the landscape alters out of all recognition. The waste materials from man's industries now begin to poison his environment. In some areas vast stretches of water have become biologically dead. Lake Erie in North America is an example of a lake suffering from eutrophication, that is, it contains far too much organic material. Sewage and industrial waste containing animal poisons and excess plant food have been flowing into the lake for a hundred years. Near the big cities large areas of the lake are unsafe to bathe in, popular species of gamefish have disappeared and the water is little more than a fluid rubbish dump. The same thing is happening in Lake Geneva and even in Loch Leven in Scotland because the rain is washing into it excess mineral fertilizers from the surrounding farmland. Even where the fish have not died, they are sometimes considered unsafe for human consumption because their bodies are full of insecticides such as DDT.

Other sources of pollution include exhaust gases from motor vehicles, which contain lead and carbon monoxide, oil slicks from disabled tankers, which kill off innumerable wild animals round the coasts of the world, poisonous crop sprays and nuclear fallout. Although it is very expensive, practical steps can be taken to cut down the amount of pollution, but this becomes more and more difficult as the population continues to grow. Clearly something must be done soon.

Fantasy or fact?

World-wide pollution

Organic mercury from a nitrogen factory in Japan accumulates in a pool, causing illness in the area.

Damage to marine life from oil has been dramatically demonstrated by tanker disasters such as that of the *Torrey Canyon*, beached off Cornwall in 1967. Equally dangerous is pollution caused by drums of toxic chemicals washed overboard from cargo ships.

Travel for some, noise for many.
Government decisions to ban night jet
flights can ease the problem. The
major sources of unnacceptable noise
are still aircraft and motor traffic.

If domestic rubbish continues to
increase at the present rate a family
using one dustbin a week will fill
five times as many — 260 dustbins in
a year — within twenty years.

Lead in the atmosphere comes mostly
from car exhausts. Research is being
carried out into the effect of this
pollution by using guinea pigs in a
cage above a motorway.

Are concrete trees a satisfactory substitute for the real thing

Conservation

Less obvious, and more difficult to combat, is the destruction of what Dr Fraser-Darling calls the 'wilderness'. As the human population increases it has a greater and greater effect on the surrounding environment. This is not something new. Some of the extinct animals of pre-historic times may have disappeared because they were slaughtered by our Stone-Age ancestors.

The cedar forests of the Lebanon, from which Solomon imported timber for his temple, have long since been chopped down. Today, the largest remaining forest in the world, the Brazilian Matto Grosso, is being steadily cut back by man. The forest lands of the Earth help to stabilize the world environment since they remove carbon dioxide from the atmosphere and give out oxygen as they photosynthesize, helping to regulate the content of the air. As they are destroyed, they cease to carry out this function.

It is also partly an ethical question. We share this planet with millions of species of other animals and plants. Should we gradually kill them all off to make room for ourselves? Very few people have ever seen a blue whale, the largest animal that has ever lived, but should it become extinct because whale-hunters harpoon it out of existence?

Hope for the future

Unless we can control the growth of the human population, the problems of pollution and conservation will become more and more difficult to handle. New ideas for food production and political changes to provide a fairer distribution of the world's goods can reduce the problem of food shortage. New ways of organizing city life could help to cut down the stresses of overcrowding to tolerable level. Overpopulation destroys the biological environment. Awareness of this danger can prompt us to develop ways of conserving the environment. However, none of the proposed solutions to these individual problems can hope to succeed if we do not tackle the fundamental problem of cutting down the explosive increase in the number of people. In the next chapter we shall look at the question of population control.

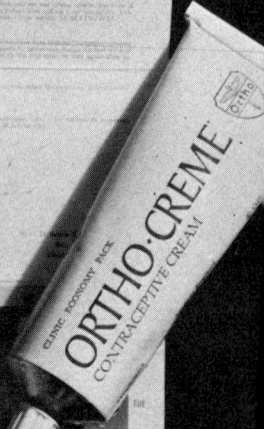

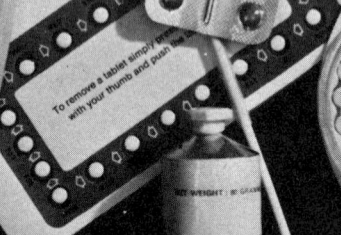

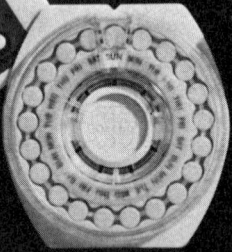

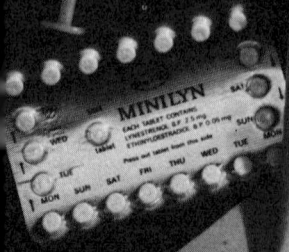

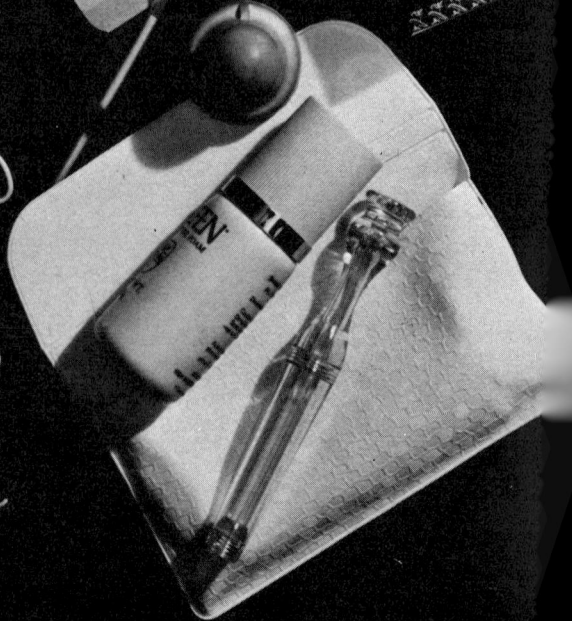

7 Population control

Increase the death-rate?

Death-control has had a remarkable effect on the growth of the human population. On the island of Mauritius, during an eight-year spell after the war, life expectancy increased from thirty-one to fifty-one years. The virtual elimination of malaria drastically reduced the death-rate, but there was no corresponding attempt to reduce the birth-rate. As more and more poverty-stricken and unproductive young people joined the population, it became impossible to use resources for planning and building up capital because most of the local produce was used to feed the growing numbers of people

In the underdeveloped parts of the world this is a typical dilemma. There are two solutions to overpopulation: either increase the death-rate or decrease the birth-rate. We will be forced to choose, if we are to avoid the nightmare absurdity of Fremlin's world in eight hundred years time. An increased death-rate could come about as the result of some universal catastrophe, perhaps nuclear war, but we hope this will not happen. Birth-control is the only humane alternative.

How is population size controlled amongst other animals, and amongst traditional human groups? Perhaps this will indicate how to tackle the problem amongst modern human societies.

Animal populations

We do not know precisely what determines the size of an animal population. There may be different causes in different species and under varying circumstances. At one end of the scale, small organisms living in harsh conditions seem to be completely at the mercy of the physical environment. For example, in the arid conditions of South Australia there are small insects called thrips which live on roses. From the rate of increase of the population and the length of the growing season, it is possible to predict very accurately what the size of the population will be at the end of the wet season.

In animals which are more independent of their physical environment, the control may be related to the density of the population. In the simplest case, when there are more animals, there is less food to go round and some starve to death. Dense populations are also more open to attack by epidemics of infectious diseases. There are other, more surprising, effects of crowding. Above a certain population density, female *Drosophila* (fruit flies) start to lay fewer eggs, and the denser the population, the fewer they lay. Flour beetles show various responses, according to the species. When the amount of flour per beetle falls below a certain level, cannibalism occurs, egg production drops, frequency of mating declines and in one species the females puncture and destroy the eggs. Some species of flour beetle have glands which release a gas when the insects become crowded. This gas is poisonous to the larvae and stops the adults mating. As we saw, in rat populations crowding reduced the rate of growth of the population even when there was plenty of food and water available. This seemed to be due to abnormal changes in behaviour and the functioning of the reproductive organs.

Wynne-Edwards's theory

In one hour an adult beaver can cut down a poplar tree big enough to feed a family of beavers for several days. A tree of this size would probably have been growing for twenty years before it was felled. So if tree growth in any one area is to keep pace with the beavers' requirements, no more than about one stem in seven thousand should be cut down on an average day. This will allow a twenty-year rotation to occur. In such a situation, food will always seem to be available in vast quantities, even though the beavers are in fact eating the equivalent of all the new growth in the forest.

If the numbers of beavers increased to the point where they were eating the poplars more quickly than they were being replaced, this would lead to an acute food shortage. Competition for food between members of the beaver population would allow the stronger to outlive the weaker, and numbers would be progressively reduced. Unfortunately the reduction in numbers would be too late, because the food supply would have been hopelessly reduced even before any of the animals died.

This type of problem led Professor V. C. Wynne-Edwards of Aberdeen University to suggest a new theory of population control. He believes that, instead of competing directly for food, many animals take part in conventional competition which limits numbers before food supplies become over-used. For example, many birds and mammals show territorial behaviour. The male red grouse tries to claim a territory of a certain minimum area which will be big enough to provide food for his dependents during the breeding season. Birds which cannot obtain a territory either do not or cannot breed. In years when the food supply is good, the grouse sets up smaller territories than in poor years, and more are able to produce offspring. Competition has been for an area of ground instead of food itself, so that if the standard territory is large enough to feed a family, the whole group will survive.

Many sea-birds do not defend a territory on the sea, but defend a nesting site on the shore, representing breeding rights. Often the site is only a few square feet, but the total colony is limited in area and any birds not obtaining a site inside the boundary do not breed.

One of Wynne-Edwards's most interesting and controversial suggestions is that competition can become extremely abstract. Male mammals often seem to fight for breeding rights, but they very seldom damage each other seriously. Wynne-Edwards believes that the dawn and dusk choruses of birds, of tropical frogs and cicadas (tropical insects) indicate the population density. According to the numbers of animals taking part, the volume of noise puts a changing pressure on the population. If the stress is great enough, numbers of animals will leave the group, reducing the population.

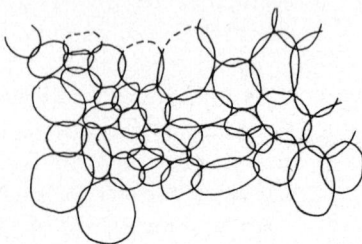

1958

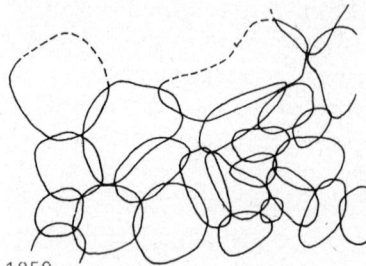

1959

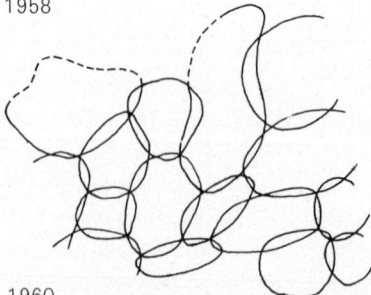

1960

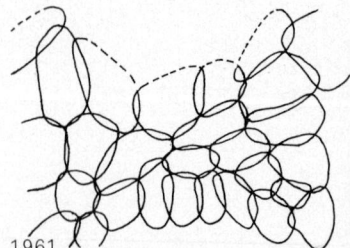

1961

The drawings show the sizes of the territories claimed by Scottish red grouse on the same piece of moorland in four successive springs. In 1958 there was plenty of food (heather) available and each male only claimed a small territory. In 1960 though, the heather was poor and each male claimed a much larger piece of territory on which to raise a family. This meant that fewer offspring were produced when there was little food available—a form of population control.

Gannets in this breeding colony have a piece of territory which they will defend as a nesting site.

Two male Impala fight over breeding rights.

Population control in traditional peoples

Population control among animals is regulated by automatic biological mechanisms. But modern civilized man's fertility can be controlled by conscious and deliberate choice. Apart from being unique in this way, the human population is also unique in showing a long-term upward acceleration in growth. Most other animals seem to maintain a relatively stable population size, and even the large changes in numbers of animals like the snowshoe hare vary about a mean value.

In the past, human societies seem to have kept their numbers fairly stable. Some evidence for this is the fact that the tools and weapons used by primitive man remained the same over many thousands of years, suggesting that they successfully adjusted to the environment. Their economy depended entirely on local food resources obtained by simple methods. If they were like modern tribal societies, they probably observed very strict territorial limits.

Some population biologists explain the stability of these tribes in Malthus's terms, saying that as the population increases, more people die of starvation, but when food is plentiful fewer people die. These traditional groups must therefore spend a good deal of time on the edge of disaster. Another view is that men in these tribes do have a vague, sometimes unconscious, knowledge of the relationship between population size and available food. Although they cannot foresee droughts or other catastrophes, they do make allowance for the times of the year when food is likely to be short.

Most societies try actively to maintain equilibrium and do not passively accept the controls of famine or disease which Malthus described. The social controls used in tribal societies, however, may be almost as automatic as biological forces. These controls are of three types: infanticide, abortion and prevention of marriage or sexual intercourse.

Infanticide

The killing of newborn infants occurs widely throughout the world and seems to have been

A fanciful eighteenth-century illustration of infanticide as practised by the natives of Florida.

universal before the advent of Christianity.
Many Australian, American and African tribes
kill off a very high proportion of their offspring
in this way, sometimes more than half of all children born. The infants are buried alive, abandoned or knocked on the head. In some tribes it
is the formal duty of one member of the family,
for example the grandfather, to decide whether
a child shall live. It is quite clear in many cases
that this is related to survival. In the Narrinyeri
tribe in Australia, every child born before the
one which preceded it could walk was destroyed, because the mother was regarded as incapable of carrying two.

Abortion

Ninety-nine per cent of all societies known to
anthropologists practise abortion, and it may
well be the commonest method of birth-
control. In pre-Christian Europe it was legal
and practised by the Greeks and Romans.

"ABORTIONS..."

R.COBB

Prevention of marriage or sexual intercourse

In most tribes young men are not allowed to
marry unless they have reached a required level
of physical fitness or skill. This is to make sure
that they will be able to maintain a family at an
acceptable standard of living. In general, men
who are inefficient or physically weak do not
marry. In some cases marriage is by purchase or
service. The prospective husband must have
collected enough wealth to be able to pay a sum
of money to the bride's father, or alternatively,
as Jacob did, according to the Old Testament,
work as a hired servant for his prospective
father-in-law, in payment for his bride. Often,
after marriage, there are taboos on sexual intercourse at particular times. Among the Bantu it

is common for intercourse to be banned for two
years after the birth of a child.

By methods such as these, populations are
kept at an acceptable level, or even at a level
which could be described as underpopulation.
Dr Mary Douglas believes that many social
controls on population size are related more to
the obtaining of social status or prestige than to
the availability of food. For example, among
the Nambudiri Brahmins of Southern India,
only the eldest son and one daughter are allowed to marry. The other sons are allowed to find
consolation with women of lower caste by using
them as concubines, but the daughters spend
the whole of their lives as secluded spinsters.
In this case, a rich landowning group has
worked out a way to avoid dividing its estates.

Newborn baby abandoned

A baby girl only a few hours old was found abandoned on a doorstep in Oxford at the weekend. She was wrapped in white, curtain-type material and a blanket had been placed in a shopping bag.

She weighs $7\frac{1}{2}$ pounds and has blue eyes and light hair. At the intensive care unit at Radcliffe Infirmary, Oxford, staff have christened her Helen.

Napoleon set up Foundling Hospitals for unwanted children which had an entrance with a revolving box so that parents could leave children without being seen. In spite of adoption, our society still has the problem of abandoned children.

People in modern society

We have seen that traditional peoples have often developed conventional ways of population control, thus preventing the action of the ultimate checks described by Malthus. In some ways they resemble the conventional competition which Wynne-Edwards believes to occur in animals. What happens in more complex societies?

In traditional European society, controls rather similar to those used by primitive people used to operate. For example, in the second half of the nineteenth century, the average completed family size for Polish peasants was proportional to the size of the farm. Peasants with no land had on average 3·9 children, whilst on farms covering more than seven hectares the average number of children was 9·1. The most important explanation for this difference is that landless peasants married much later than their richer neighbours. The Southern Irish of today tend to marry very late or not at all. Traditionally the youngest son maintains the farm, cares for his parents and usually does not marry while

they are alive. As a result, population growth is very slow in spite of the condemnation of contraception in Ireland. During the Christian era, celibacy and postponement of marriage took over from infanticide and abortion as the socially accepted means of population control in Europe. In fact, during the seventeenth century, Bavaria even had legislation to forbid the marriage of the poor.

Nevertheless, behind the scenes both infanticide and abortion have been very common. During the late eighteenth century and the nineteenth century, infanticide was almost institutionalized in Europe, via the foundling hospitals which looked after abandoned infants. These hospitals had a scandalous mortality record, the figures for some of the Italian hospitals being between 80 and 90 per cent deaths of all infants admitted. The practice of abandoning children was so common in France, even among the well-to-do, that in 1811 Napoleon ordered that foundling hospitals should have a turntable device installed so that mothers should not have the embarrassment of being

'Pregnant' men campaign for free contraception in the London borough of Newham.

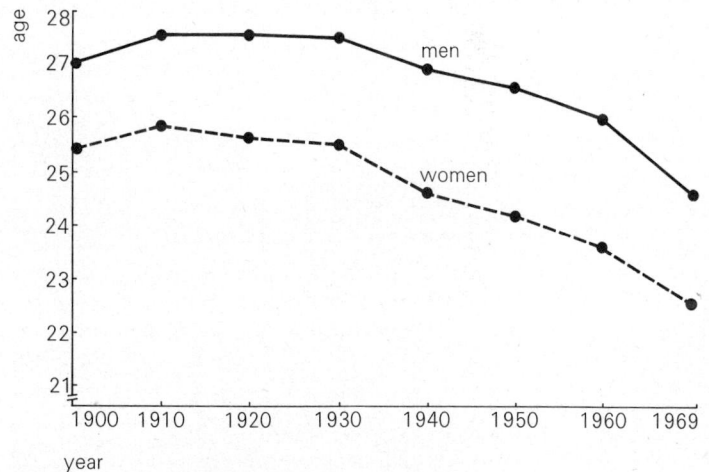

seen by the hospital staff when they abandoned their child. Today abortions are very common and estimates for the 1960s in the United States, where there are strict anti-abortion laws, are between seven hundred thousand and two million annually. The laws against abortion in many countries, though, are now being gradually relaxed.

The two greatest hopes for a morally acceptable and realistic approach to population control are the spread of contraceptive information and devices, and voluntary sterilization. There is no doubt that the low growth-rate for the populations of the advanced industrial nations is almost entirely due to the widespread use of contraceptives. In countries suffering because of population growth, attempts are being made to implement national birth-control policies either by publicizing and making available contraceptive devices or by offering free sterilization to people who do not want more children.

The average age at first marriage in England and Wales has been steadily dropping since 1930. Because of the increased use of contraception, this has had little effect on the birth-rate.

Some problems

There are few objections made against death-control. However, attempts to control fertility have not been very successful yet. This is due partly to opposition from those who believe contraception is immoral and partly to ignorance and poverty.

Conservationists believe that the exploitation of natural resources should always be less than the maximum possible. If Wynne-Edwards is correct, most animals have evolved methods of population control to achieve this. Something very similar seems to happen among traditional human groups, but in modern nations, especially those which are economically underdeveloped, the old social controls do not seem to have survived or to have been replaced. We know of many methods of birth-control, but these are worthless if people either refuse or cannot afford to use them.

It has been said that the population explosion cannot be controlled until there is world-wide agreement to disarm, so that the billions of dollars spent on weapons could be used to raise the living standards of the poor. Birth-control methods are used widely only by literate and reasonably fed people who have some hope of improving their lot and that of their children. At the moment this level of education and prosperity has not been reached in the poor countries.

Wild animals completely obey the social code, even when this means they must not breed, or they are pushed out of the community or die. Man has much greater personal independence, and because of this he is creative and can solve complex problems far beyond the powers of other animals. Consequently he is also free to solve, or not to solve, the problem of population control in his own species. It is up to him to decide.

The Indian government has launched a nation-wide family-planning campaign to tackle the enormous population problems. Elephants are used to give away free contraceptives and any male who undergoes sterilization is given a cash reward. Information and advice can be seen everywhere.

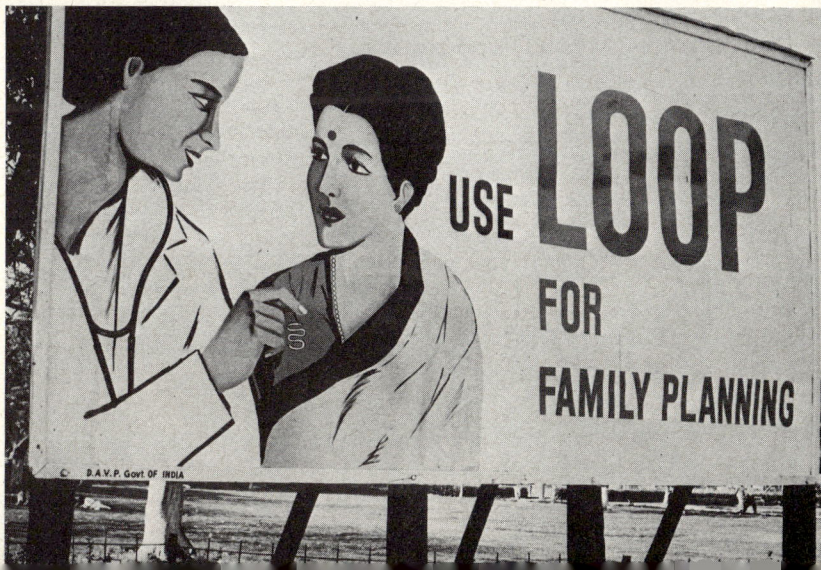

Methods of contraception

Method		Pregnancies among 100 women in one year	How it is used
The pill	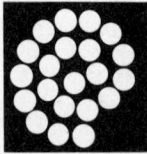	virtually none	The woman takes the pill regularly (usually every night for three weeks, followed by one week break. It varies with type).
Coil (IUD)		2–3	The IUD is a plastic coil that is placed in the womb. It must be fitted by a doctor first and then left there undisturbed.
Safe period or Rhythm method		5 or more	The woman keeps a calendar on which she marks her daily body temperature. The temperature graph predicts times when conception is most likely, and intercourse is avoided at these times.
Spermicides: creams, jellies and aerosols		5 or more	The woman puts some of the spermicide in her vagina before intercourse takes place.
Condom	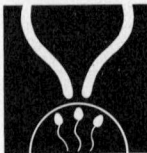	2–3	The condom (French letter or durex) is a rubber sheath that is rolled on to the penis before intercourse.
Cap		2–3	The cap is a rubber dome (diaphragm) that the woman places over the entrance to the womb before intercourse.
Withdrawal and holding back		5 or more	
Sterilization	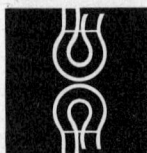	none	

How it works	Comments
The pill contains hormones that stop the release and implanting of the egg (ovum).	There may be some side-effects such as headaches but a change of brand can often remove these problems. There is also a slight risk of thrombosis, but this is less than the risk involved in being pregnant. When they stop taking the pill, women are as fertile as before.
The coil probably stops the fertilized egg implanting in the wall of the womb.	The coil is only suitable for women who have already had children. In some women the coil may cause heavy periods. Fertility is unaffected when the coil is removed.
Conception can occur only when there is an egg (ovum) in the womb. One egg is released every month about 14 days after a period. There is a change in average body temperature following the release of an egg, and knowledge of this indicates when intercourse is unsafe.	Women with irregular periods do not find this method very reliable.
These all contain a substance that can kill the sperm.	They should not be used on their own but with other methods, such as the condom or the cap. Aerosol sprays are the most effective of the spermicides.
It stops any sperm that the man produces entering the woman. It is best to use a spermicide with the condom.	This method does not require medical advice and is the most popular. The pill is more effective, though.
It stops the sperm entering the womb and is used with a spermicide.	It must be fitted by a doctor in the first place. There are no side-effects.
Withdrawal – the man removes his penis from the woman's vagina before he releases any sperm (ejaculates). Holding back—the man has no climax at all and releases no sperm.	Neither of these is very effective and both are very unsatisfying.
In men, the tube that carries the sperm is cut. In women, the tube that eggs pass through is cut.	These operations are simple to carry out but not normally reversible. People who are sterilized must be sure that they want no more children. Sexual pleasure is not affected by sterilization and there are no side effects.

Workers in Morocco enjoy a traditional tea ceremony. Industrialization will force them to make great changes in their way of life.

8 Industrial populations

We have looked at some of the ways in which biological factors affect human population growth. Two important things have become clear. Firstly, we do not know all the answers. Although there are many interesting theories to account for differences in birth-rates, death-rates and migration, and how the human population remained relatively stable in the past, there is not enough evidence available to make us feel very confident about more than a few of them. This evidence needs to be collected. Secondly, although biological laws underlie all the phenomena of population, once societies reach an advanced level of technology and culture it is more meaningful to explain what is happening in terms of sociological, economic and political influences.

The study of population statistics in themselves is called *demography*. All advanced countries now collect detailed statistics on births, marriages and deaths, and every few years a census of the population is taken. In England these figures are published by the General Register Office in London. World figures for population changes are much more difficult to compile because many underdeveloped countries do not keep complete records. However, a very detailed list of the available statistics is published every year in the United Nations Demographic Yearbook.

ne lonely worker controls a whole battery of machines. Industrialization changes e work pattern of a country, often reducing the number of jobs available rather an providing the employment needed by underdeveloped countries.

Surrounding every South American city are villages of hastily built shacks. In this one (above) outside Brazilia, the capital of Brazil, nearly half of the city's population live without water or electricity. In the background are buildings containing government departments. Squatters (right) outside Lima, Peru are not even allowed to build such feeble shelters, but are driven away.

Transition theory

From a careful study of these figures, demographers have worked out a description of what they think happened in the history of the population of a modern industrial nation. Throughout most of human history, they believe, man has had a very high death-rate and a high birth-rate. The death-rate may have been due to infanticide, epidemic disease or starvation, but it was typical of traditional tribal and peasant societies. Since it was balanced by large numbers of births, the size of the population remained stable. Modern populations in Africa, and much of South America and Asia, are examples of what may have been universal in the past. In these countries, a very large proportion of the population belongs to an age-group capable of becoming parents. This means that, compared with modern industrial countries, the birth-rate will be very high, not only because women have bigger families, but because the proportion of women capable of having children is also much higher.

This is a stage of high potential growth because, if the death-rate could be reduced, the population would increase very rapidly. In about one-fifth of the world, modern medicine has reduced the death-rate and here the population explosion is greatest. South-eastern Europe, some South American countries and India are all more or less at this stage. It seems almost certain that many more countries will arrive at this situation by the end of the century. The available statistics suggest that the modern industrial nations of the West passed through a phase like this in the nineteenth century.

An age pyramid is a way of showing the proportions of the population in each age group. The age pyramid for India in 1931 is very similar to that for England in 1841, with the youngest age range containing the largest number of people in both cases, and a fairly steady decline in numbers to the ninety to ninety-five age range.

After this transitional growth stage, a third change took place in the Western nations. The birth-rate began to drop, and by the 1930s several North European countries had reached a new stable level with low birth-rates combined with low death-rates. In some countries the population declined, and governments actively encouraged people to have more children.

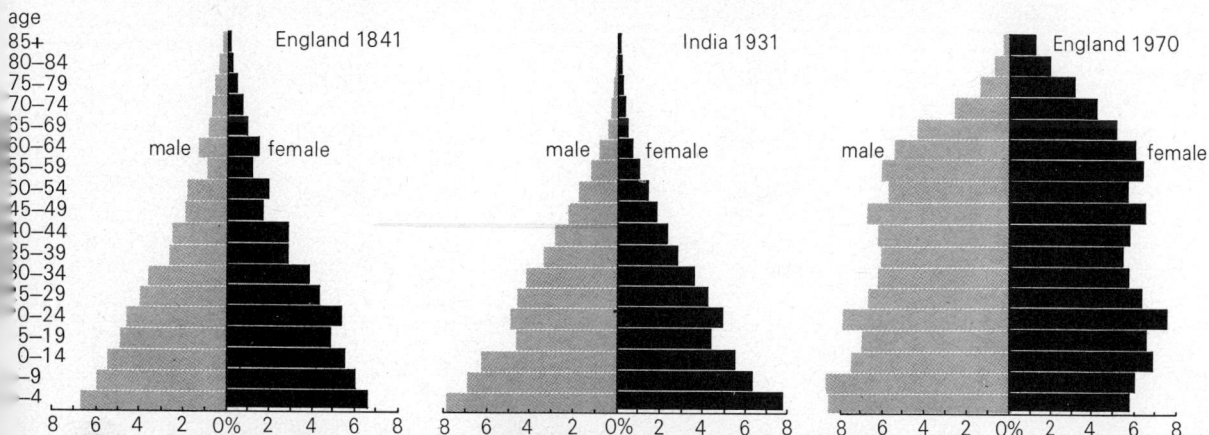

The age pyramid for England in 1841 is very like that for India in 1931. The broad bases of the pyramids show that both populations were increasing rapidly. The age pyramid for England in 1970 is typical of a society that has been industrialized for a long time. A reasonably constant birth rate and a low death rate in early and middle age result in a rectangular shape that tapers off at the top as people die of old age.

The three stages in this transition can be summarized in a graph. Each has a distinctive economic arrangement. In the earliest phase there is a very low level of productivity, energy sources are primitive, and the standard of living is very low. At the middle stage, agriculture becomes more productive but does not always keep up with population growth, and industrial growth begins. The third stage has a very high standard of living, great efficiency and universal, sophisticated technology.

This 'transition' theory of population growth is based on what happened in modern industrial nations. If the theory is applicable to the underdeveloped countries, we would expect that if they industrialize and modernize there will be a decline in fertility until the population is stabilized. If industrialization is not achieved in the next one hundred years there are two other possibilities for slowing the growth of the population. The death-rate could begin to rise again because medicine and hygiene cannot keep up with the continued rise in population. Alternatively, there could be a decline in fertility before industrialization. This has never happened before, but it is just possible that a peasant population might be influenced by a widespread birth-control campaign if they had enough help and encouragement from the government.

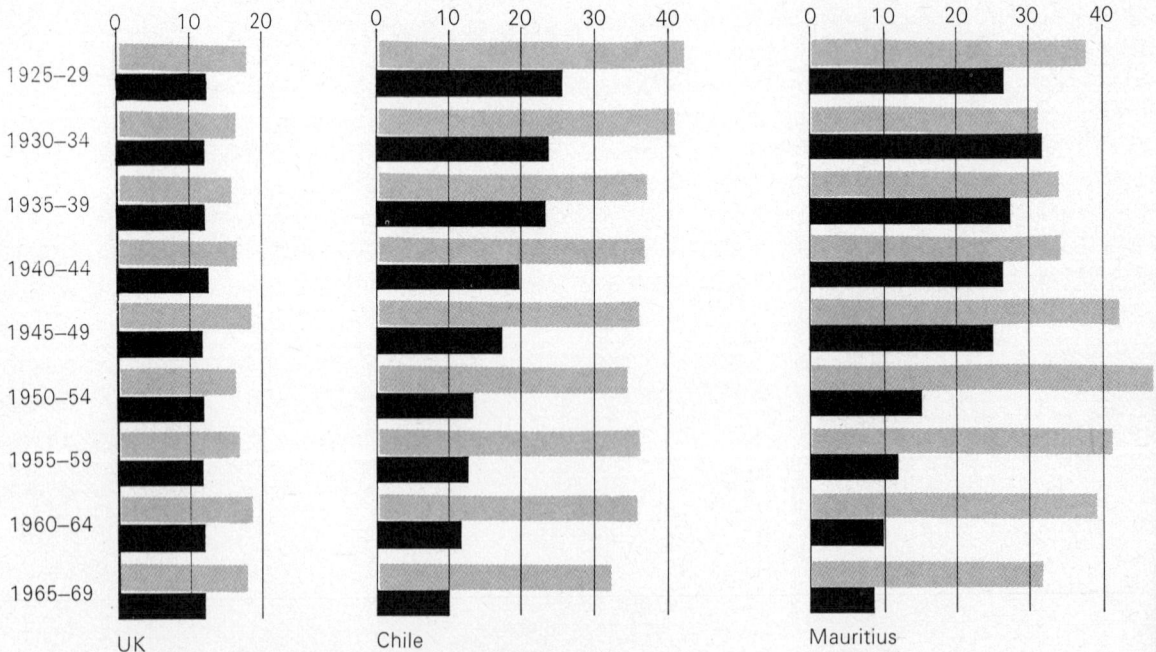

In underdeveloped countries such as Chile and Mauritius the birth-rates (grey) have remained high, whilst the death-rates (black) have declined dramatically – this has caused a large increase in the population. In the UK, both the birth-rate and the death-rate have remained relatively low over the past fifty years.

The transition theory

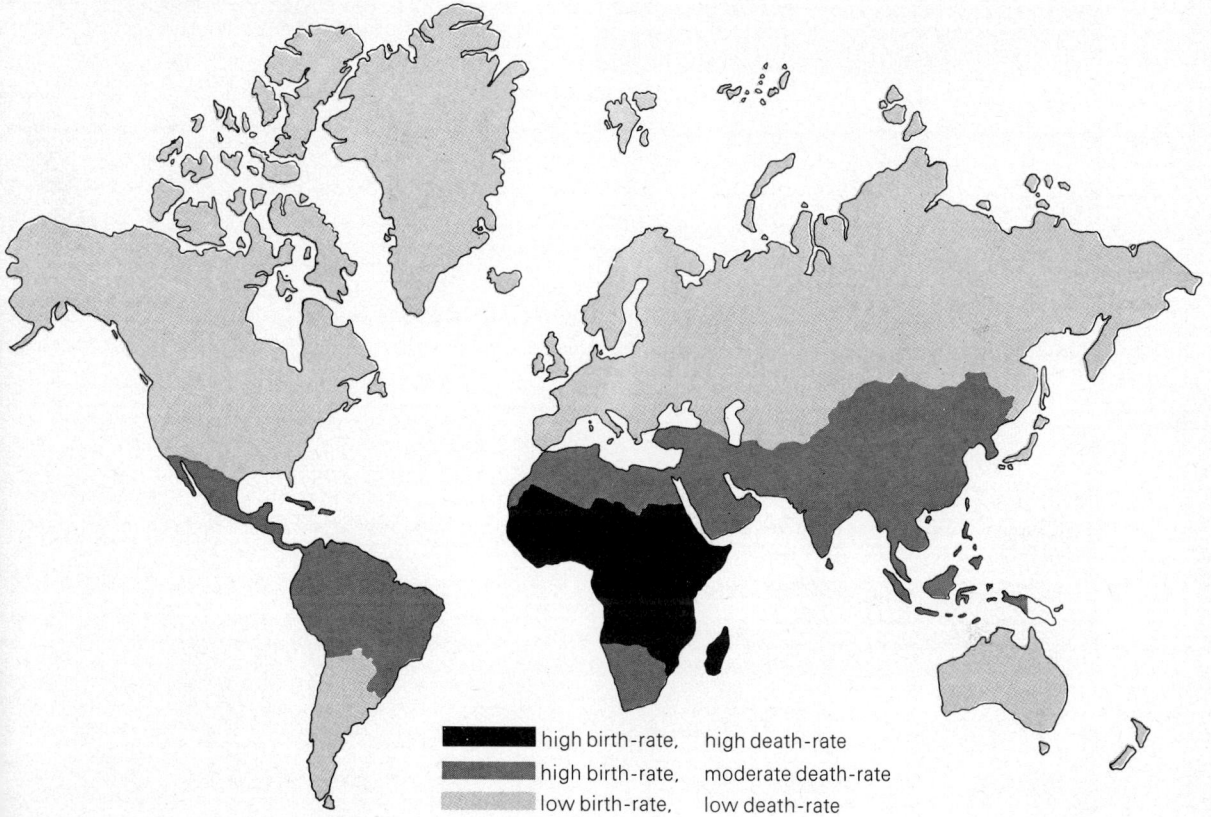

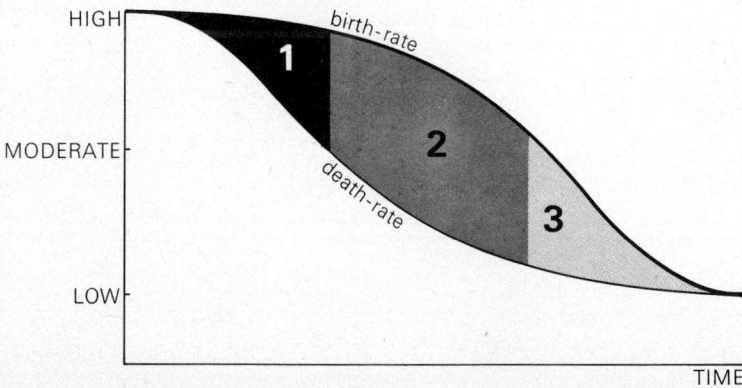

high birth-rate, high death-rate
high birth-rate, moderate death-rate
low birth-rate, low death-rate

The graph illustrates the three stages in the transition to an industrial society. The map, prepared by the United Nations, forecasts which of these stages various regions of the world will have reached by 1975.

London

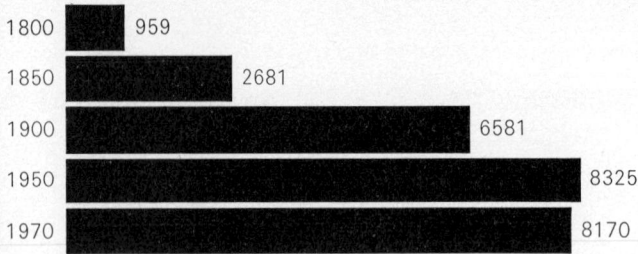

Year	Population
1800	959
1850	2681
1900	6581
1950	8325
1970	8170

New York

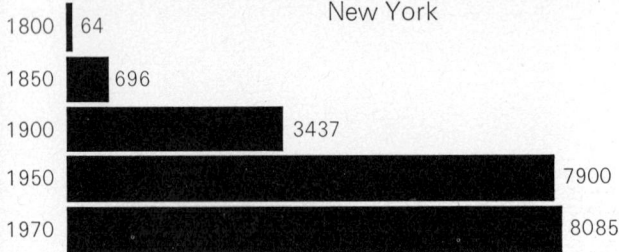

Year	Population
1800	64
1850	696
1900	3437
1950	7900
1970	8085

Tokyo

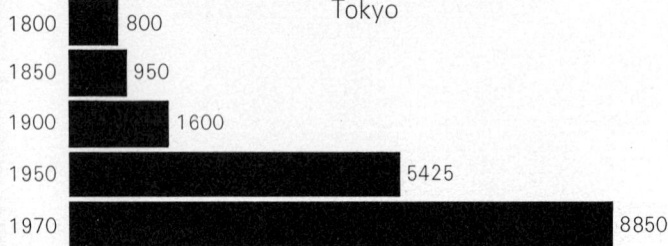

Year	Population
1800	800
1850	950
1900	1600
1950	5425
1970	8850

Moscow

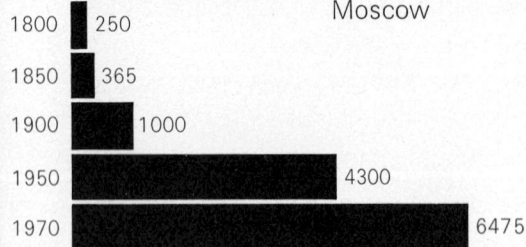

Year	Population
1800	250
1850	365
1900	1000
1950	4300
1970	6475

Buenos Aires

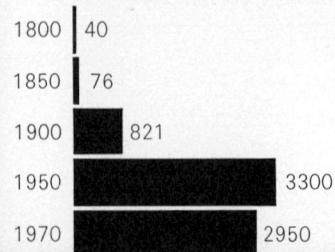

Year	Population
1800	40
1850	76
1900	821
1950	3300
1970	2950

figures in thousands

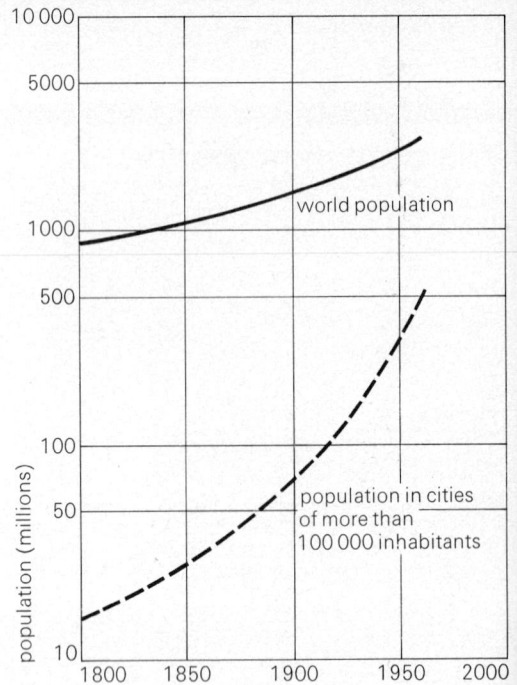

world population

population in cities
of more than
100 000 inhabitants

population (millions)

In 1800 there were only six cities in the whole of the United States with a population of 8000 or more. Today over 13 per cent of the world's population live in cities with 100 000 inhabitants or more. The graph shows that the number of people living in cities with a population of over 100 000 is increasing much faster than the total population of the world — more and more people are moving to and living in cities.

Some criticisms

Recently, doubts have been raised about this transition theory. Firstly, there is the anthropological evidence which has been collected in the debate on Wynne-Edwards' theory of population control (page 72), and whether it is applicable to man. Among simple tribes, conventional practices, such as taboos on sexual intercourse for certain ages, which lower the fertility of the population, are widespread if not universal. It is therefore possible that very high birth-rates with balancing death-rates were not always found in traditional societies.

Secondly, increasing industrialization may not, in fact, always be combined with decreasing fertility. Since 1945, fertility in the United States has increased and remained above the level it was just before the Second World War. This is in spite of the fact that there had also been a dramatic increase in economic development. Historical studies have shown that the fertility of the English population went up, rather than declined, during the Industrial Revolution.

Perhaps we should distinguish between the direct and the indirect effects of industrial development. The direct effect of increased wealth may be an increase in fertility, but in the long term there has usually been a decline. This is probably due to social factors like increased education, knowledge of contraception, ambitions for a higher standard of living and so on.

These decisions about the size of the family have obviously been conscious ones. Maybe there is room for guarded optimism about the future. Disaster is not inevitable, but there is very little time to educate the whole of mankind and provide economic and social incentives, to halt the staggering population growth.

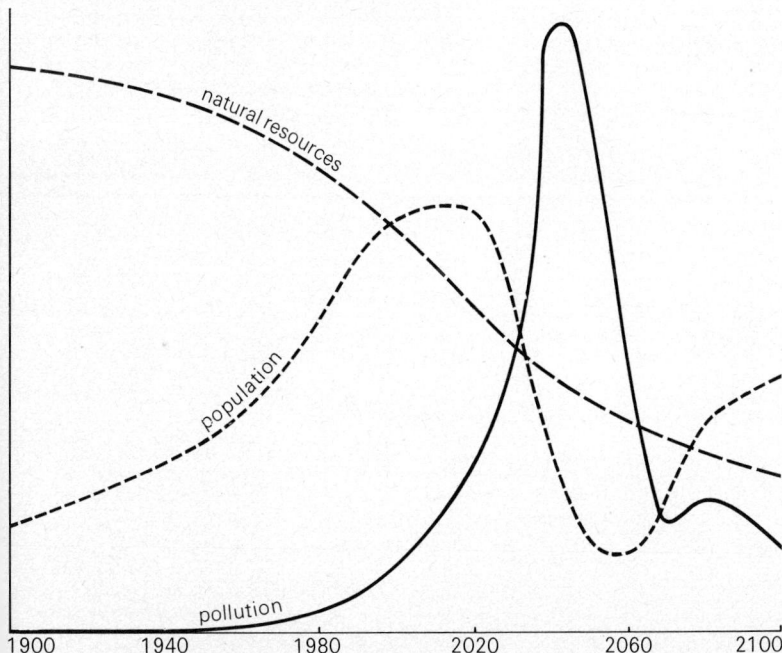

A sample prediction, by a computer at the Massachusetts Institute of Technology of the problems the world will have to face if the population continues to grow. The computer predicts that we will use up most of our natural resources and cause more and more pollution until there is a 'disaster' – a huge collapse in population just after 2020 AD.

Further information

Bibliography

There are a great number of books on population and its related problems. Many of these are written at quite a high level and are more suitable for use as reference and are marked ■. Some are well suited for younger readers and are marked □. The list is by no means comprehensive, but many of the sources listed can supply further information and ideas.

Human population growth

■ B. Benjamin, *The Population Census* (Heinemann, 1970). Looks at the development of the census in Great Britain and examines the various questions asked.
■ W. D. Borrie, *The Growth and Control of World Populations* (Weidenfeld & Nicholson, 1970).
■ A. M. Carr-Saunders, *World Population* (Oxford University Press, 1936).
□ C. Cipolla, *The Economic History of World Population*, 5th edn (Penguin, 1970).
■ P. Ehrlich, *The Population Bomb* (Pan, 1971).
■ G. Hardin, *Population, Evolution and Birth Control* (W. H. Freeman, 1969). Contains over 100 controversial articles, including J. H. Fremlin's 'How many people can the world support?'
■ R. K. Kelsall, *Population* (Longman, 1967).
■ P. Laslett, *The World We Have Lost* (Methuen, 1965). An interesting book on social history up to 1850. It considers the effect of plague on population, age of marriage, etc.
■ T. R. Malthus, *An Essay on the Principle of Population* (Penguin, 1970).
□ C. W. Park, *The Population Explosion* (Heinemann, 1969). Intended for liberal studies use.
■ *The Population Explosion – an Interdisciplinary Approach* (Open University Press, 1971).
■ T. K. Robinson, *The Population of Britain* (Longman, for the Institute of Economic Affairs, 1968). A useful source of information but intended for sixth-form work.
■ L. R. Taylor (ed.), *The Optimum Population for Britain* (Academic Press, 1970).
■ C. D. Williams, *Population Problems in Developing Countries* (IPPF, 1969). Available from VCOAD.
■ E. A. Wrigley, *Population and History* (Weidenfeld & Nicholson, 1969). Well-illustrated, but text is rather difficult.

Population and food

■ G. Borgstram, *Too Many* (Collier-Macmillan, 1969). A useful discussion of the limits of food production.
■ N. Calder, *The Environment Game* (Secker & Warburg, 1967; Panther, 1969).
■ F. F. Darling, *Wilderness and Plenty* (BBC Publications, 1970; Pan, 1971). The 1969 Reith Lectures.
■ R. Dumont and R. Bernard, *The Hungry Future* (Deutsch, 1969). Looks at the problems of feeding the population of the Third World.
□ N. L. Fyson, Food (Batsford, 1972). Well-illustrated with photographs.
□ J. H. Lowry, *World Population and Food Supply* (Edward Arnold, 1970). Well-illustrated; intended for geographers.
□ A. McKenzie, *The Hungry World* (Faber, 1969). A small book which covers most of the ground in an easy text with line illustrations.
□ M. Morgan, *Population and Food Supply* (Collins, 1969). An illustrated topic book.
■ N. W. Pirie, *Food Resources* (Penguin, 1969).

Population and the environment

■ J. Barr (ed.), *Environmental Handbook* (Pan, 1970).
■ H. Brown, *The Challenge of Man's Future* (Viking Press, 1954). A classic work on population and resources.
■ B. Commoner, *Science and Survival* (Viking Press, 1967).
■ R. F. Dasmann, *Planet in Peril* (Penguin–Unesco, 1972).
□ P. R. and A. H. Ehrlich, *Population,*

Resources, Environment: Issues in Human Ecology, 2nd edn (W. H. Freeman, 1972). A source book.
■ P. Gresswell, *Environment: An Alphabetical Handbook* (Murray, 1971).
□ J. Joffe, *Conservation* (Aldus, 1969). Many full-colour illustrations.
□ J. A. Lauwery, *Man's Impact on Nature* (Aldus, 1969). Many full-colour illustrations.
■ D. H. Meadows *et al.*, *The Limits to Growth* (Earth Island, 1972). A report for the Club of Rome's project on the predicament of mankind.
■ K. Mellanby, *Pesticides and Pollution* (Fontana, 1969).
■ M. Nicholson, *The Environmental Revolution* (Hodder & Stoughton, 1970; Penguin, 1972).
□ K. Reid, *Nature's Networks* (Aldus, 1969). Many full-colour illustrations.
■ B. Ward and R. Dubos, *Only One Earth* (Deutsch; Penguin, 1972).
■ The Ecologist, *Blueprint for Survival* (Penguin, 1972).

Population control

□ A. Allison (ed.), *Population Control* (Penguin, 1970).
□ Consumers Association, *Contraceptives a Which?* Supplement (Consumer Association, 1970). Excellent survey and evaluation of all methods of contraception available.
□ R. J. Demarest and J. Sciarra, *Conception, Birth and Contraception* (Hodder & Stoughton, 1969).
□ E. Draper, *Birth Control in the Modern World*, 2nd edn (Penguin, 1972).
□ E. Haveman, *Birth Control* (Time–Life, International & Seymour Press, 1967). A well-written book with many good photographs.
■ J. A. Loraine, *Sex and the Population Crises* (Heinemann , 1970).
■ J. Medawar and D. Pyke (eds.), *Family Planning* (Penguin, 1971).
□ W. B. Pomeroy, *Boys and Sex* (Delacourte Press, 1968; Penguin, 1970).

□ W. B. Pomeroy, *Girls and Sex* (Delacourte Press, 1969; Penguin, 1971).
■ P. Vaughan, *Pill on Trial* (Weidenfeld & Nicholson, 1970; Penguin, 1972).
□ C. Wood, *Birth Control – Now and Tomorrow* (Peter Davies, 1969).

Social considerations

■ M. Allaby, *The Eco-Activists* (Charles Knight, 1971).
■ C. Clark, *Population Control and Land Use* (Macmillan, 1967).
□ N. L. Fyson, *The Development Puzzle* (available from VCOAD). A very valuable source book for teaching about the 'rich world–poor world' divide.
□ W. J. Hanson, *Hongkong: The Overcrowded Room* (Longman, 1969). No. 9 in set C of the Longman Oxfam Series.
■ D. Lawton (ed.), *Population Education and the Younger Education* (IPPF, 1971). A very practical book on teaching about population. Contains a bibliography.
■ Schools Council General Studies Project, Unit on *Population* (Longman–Penguin, 1972). Details from Publishing Manager, General Studies Project, The Kings Manor, York.
■ Scientific American, *Science, Conflict and Society* (W. H. Freeman, 1969). Readings from *Scientific American*; there are a number of articles on population, including one by Wynne-Edwards.

Booklets, pamphlets and topic folders

Many of the organizations noted below can provide booklets, factsheets, etc, on population problems. Particularly useful are:
Man's Population Predicament: a booklet published by the Population Reference Bureau Inc, Washington D.C. Includes useful graphs. Available from VCOAD.
Falling Birth-Rates and Family Planning: Duplicated sheets on sixteen countries with falling birth-rates. Free from VCOAD, who can supply a complete list of materials.

Why Britain needs a Population Policy: from the Conservation Society.

Topic folders from VCOAD. Nine folders on topics such as population, education and health. Each contains information sheets and other materials from VCOAD and other agencies.

Population Pack: the IPPF has prepared an information pack on population and family planning designed for teachers. It contains up-to-date population statistics, a range of information on family-planning programmes around the world, bibliographies and information on teaching materials. Under £1.00. Write to IPPF for further information.

Journals and articles

Journals covering environmental health and scientific areas may contain material on population. Particularly relevant are:

The Ecologist, 73 Kew Green, Richmond, Surrey.

BEE (Bulletin of Environmental Education) from the Environmental Education Unit, TCPA, 17 Carlton House Terrace, London SW1.

Your Environment, 10 Roderick Road, London NW3 (especially no 5, December 1970, 'The People Plague').

Scientific American

National Geographic Magazine

The following articles might also be useful:

R. M. Adams, 'The Origin of Cities', *Scientific American*, September 1960.

R. H. Braidwood, 'The Agricultural Revolution', *Scientific American*, September 1960.

J. B. Calhain, 'Population Density and Social Pathology', *Scientific American*, February 1962.

G. Chedd, 'Famine or Sanity', *New Scientist*, 23 October 1969.

K. Davis, 'Population', *Scientific American*, September 1963.

E. S. Deevey, 'The Human Population' *Scientific American*, September 1960.

W. Mangin, 'Squatter Settlements', *Scientific American*, October 1967.

R. N. Tiennes, 'Stress in a Crowded World', *New Scientist*, 19 September 1963.

V. C. Wynne-Edwards, 'Population Control in Animals', *Scientific American*, August 1964.

Addresses of organizations

The following are all active in the area of population education and can supply information about their activities.

Birth Control Campaign, 233 Tottenham Court Road, London W1.

CA Publications, Christian Aid, PO Box 1, 2 Sloane Gardens, London SW1.

CS, Conservation Society, 21 Hanyards Lane, Cuffley, Potters Bar, Hertfordshire.

Commonwealth Institute, Kensington High Street, London W8.

IPPF, International Planned Parenthood Federation, Information Department, 18–20 Lower Regent Street, London SW1. (Library open to public.)

ITDG, Intermediate Technology Development Group, 9 King Street, London WC2.

ODI, Overseas Development Institute (10–11 Percy Street, London W1P 0JB), orders for lists and publications to Research Publications Services Ltd, 11 Nelson Road, London SE10. (Library open to public.)

OXFAM, Education Department, Oxfam, 274 Banbury Road, Oxford.

3W1, Third World First, Britwell Salome, Oxford.

UNICEF, New Gallery Centre, 123 Regent Street, London W1.

VCOAD, Education Unit, Voluntary Committee on Overseas Aid and Development, 69 Victoria Street, London SW1.

WOW, War on Want, 28 The Grove, London W5.

Games

Most of the population games available are American. More information about classroom use of these materials, lists of games and bibliographies can be found in the books mentioned.

The Aid Committee Game – players study one

developing country and its problems and decide what projects to support. From Oxfam Education Department.

The Development Game – from Oxfam Education Department.

Galapagos (Evolution). A simulation of the evolution of Darwin's finches, in which players fill a scientific role and are requested to predict the evolution rate. 6–50 players, takes 1–2 hours. From ABT Associates Inc., 14 Concord Lane, Cambridge, Massachusetts, USA.

Population. A board game designed to simulate some of the problems of over-population likely to occur in a rapidly developing country. 4 players (minimum), 1–2 hours. From Urban Systems Inc., 1033 Massachusetts Avenue, Cambridge, Massachusetts 02138, USA.

Bulletin of Environmental Education, no. 13 (May 1972) – contains a number of articles and lists of games and simulations.

C. Longley (ed.) *Games and Simulations* (BBC Publications, 1972).

R. Walford, *Games in Geography* (Longman, 1969).

Wall charts

Charting Poverty. Four charts, one on population increase. Oxfam.

Food and Agriculture Organization. Four charts on world population growth.

War on Want. Set of four charts on population growth, diet, etc. From WOW.

Population Topics. A series of wall charts produced by ILO and IPPF. Distributed by IPPF.

Pictorial discussion sheets from Oxfam. One on the population explosion.

Films and filmstrips

16mm films for hire or free loan:
And on the Eighth Day, 2 parts, each 30 min, Thames Television
Beyond Conception, 40 min, Concord
Clouds Over Paradise, 25 min, British Film Institute
Family Planning, 10 min, Concord
Food or Famine, 27 min, PFB

Kirashimo (a useful case study of Kenyan problems), 13 min, Concord
Let there be Bread, 16 min, RFL
Man and his Resources, Concord
Mauritius, 25 min, Concord
The Population Problem, 13 min, National Audio Visual Aids
Population (from a series called 'Evidence'), Thames Television
The Population Problem (series of six films), 30 min each, Concord.
A Threat or a Promise, 10 min, Concord
To Plan your Family, 14 min, Concord
The Shadow of Progress, 27 min, PFB
The Squeeze, BFI
Our Environment (filmstrip), VIS
Science and Natural Resources (filmstrip), Encyclopaedia Britannica

Addresses for films and filmstrips

Thames Television, Television House, Kingsway, London WC2.
Concord Films Council, Nacton, Ipswich, Suffolk, IP10 OJ2.
British Film Institute, 42–3 Lower Marsh Street, London SE1.
National Audio Visual Council, Paxton Place, Gipsy Road, London SE27.
PFB (Petroleum Films Bureau), 4 Brook Street, Hanover Square, London W1.
VIS (Visual Information Service Ltd) 12 Bridge Street, Hungerford, Berkshire.
Encyclopaedia Britannica International Ltd, 18–20 Lower Regent Street, London SW1.
RFL (Rank Film Library), 1 Aintree Road, Perivale, Greenford, Middlesex.

Sources of statistics

UN Demographic Yearbook. Most libraries should have a copy. This is *the* source for world-wide statistics on population and is published every year.
Registrar-General's *Statistical Review of England and Wales* (HMSO). Contains very detailed information relating to England and Wales.

Index

Aborigines 14, 15, 37, 48–55, 75
abortion 74, 75, 76, 77
accidents 27, 32
Africa 14, 22, 37, 61, 85
age pyramid 85
Agricultural Revolution 15, 17
Alaska 37
Arctic 54
Arunta 51
Asia 22, 31, 37, 38, 61, 85
Australia 17, 37, 38, 43, 49–55, 57
Aymara Indians 47

bacteria 9, 20, 57
Baja Indians 54, 55
Bangladesh 32, 36, 61
Bantu 75
baobab trees 27
Bavaria 76
bears 27
beaver 72
beetles, flour 9, 71
Bengal 32
Bering Strait 37
Biafra 32
birds 28
Birdsell 50–54
birth control 24, 35, 86
birth-rate
  crude 19–25, 33, 46, 71, 83, 85, 87
  specific 19
blood sugar 63
Brazil 38, 84
Brazilia 84
British 29, 42, 46
Bronze Age 27
buffaloes 15
bulge 33
Burma 24
Bushman 54, 55

Calcutta 17
Calhoun, John 64

Californian Desert 54
Canada 10, 38, 57
cannibalism 32, 64, 71
cancer 32
Cape Verde 27
carbon monoxide 65
census 11, 12, 13
Ceylon 35
Chile 40
China 32
Christianity 75, 76
Clark, Colin 17, 57
climate 39, 44, 60
cod 20
concentration camps 21
conservation 69, 78
contraception 24, 77–81, 89
conventional competition 72, 76
crash 10, 17
crocodiles 30
crop sprays 65
Cudmore, A. F. 50

Darwin, Charles 47
DDT 35, 65
death-rate 20, 33–6, 46, 71, 83, 85, 86, 87
de Castro, Josue 20
deer 49
Deevey, Edward S. 14, 17
Demographic Yearbook, United Nations 83
demography 83
depression 24, 38
desert 44, 55
dingo 37
disease 10, 17, 28, 31–3, 35, 44, 71, 85
Dividing Range 53
Domesday 11
d'Orbigny, Alcide 47
Douglas, Mary 75
Drakenberg, Christen 28
duck-billed platypus 37
Dutch 57, 59

East Indies 37
ecological death 32
economic influences 24, 39, 43, 46, 83, 86
Egypt 19, 20, 27, 40
Ehrlich, Paul 17
elephants 20, 27
emigration 61
Emlen, John 37
energy 15, 32
England 11, 29, 42, 83, 85, 89
Eskimos 54
Europe 17, 22, 29, 31, 35, 37, 38, 39, 43, 76, 85
eutrophication 64
evolution 28, 29

famine 32, 33
family 49
FAO 20
Far East 43
fecundity 19
fertility 18–25, 74, 86, 89
fish 28
Fisher, Sir Ronald 22
food chain 30, 52, 55
Forbes, D. 47
foundling hospitals 76
France 25, 76
Fraser-Darling, Sir Frank 69
Fremlin, J. H. 9, 60, 61, 71
fruit flies 28, 71

Gabon 29
gannet 73
General Register Office, London 83
generation time 20
Germany 42
glands 63
Greeks 27, 75
grouse, red 72
growth curve 9, 14, 17
growth-rate 9
Guinea 22, 29, 43

habitats 38
Hammond, John 21
hawks 30
Heyerdahl, Thor 38, 40, 41
hierarchy, social 37
highlands 44, 46, 47
homeostatic 20
horde 49, 64
human zoo 64
hunting and food gathering 14, 49
hydra 28

ice age 37, 38
impala 73
India 20, 32, 35, 43, 61, 75, 85
Indians, American 37, 38, 49
industrial populations 28, 34, 46, 61, 77, 85, 89
Industrial Revolution 14, 15, 22, 89
infanticide 74, 76, 85
intestinal infections 34
Ireland 32, 76
Italy 38, 42, 76

Jacob 75
Japanese 57
Java 43

Kalahari Desert 54
kangaroo 37, 50
Keys, Ancel 21
koala bear 37
Kon Tiki 38, 40, 41

Lake
 Alexandrina 53
 Erie 64
 Geneva 64
 Maracaibo 38
 Popiltah 50
landform 44, 46
language 38
Latin America 22, 61
lead 65

Lebanon 41, 69
life expectancy 28, 29
life-span 27, 28, 34
lions 27, 30
Loch Leven 64
London 31, 83
longevity 27
long-tailed shrews 49
Los Angeles 34
Lubras 50
lynx 10

MacLulich, D. A. 10
Madras 21
Mali 22
Malthus, T. R. 57, 74, 76
mallee 50
Maraura tribe 50
Massachusetts Institute of Technology 89
Matto Grosso 69
Mauritius 71
Mexico 40
mice 37
migration 36–47, 49, 83
moon 29
Morocco 40, 82
Morris, Desmond 64
mortality 26, 76
Moses 27
mummies 27
Murray–Darling River 53

Nambudiri Brahmins 75
Nanja horde 50
Napoleon 38, 76
Narrinyeri tribe 75
Niger 29
noise 67
nomadic garden culture 17
Northern Ireland 29
Norway 29, 40
New York 46
New Zealand 38, 57

Nile 41, 43, 44
Nonnia 50
North America 22, 37, 38, 43
nuclear fallout 65

oestrogens 20
oil slicks 65
optimum population 9, 61
overcrowding 10, 17, 37, 63, 64, 69
overheating 60, 61
overpopulation 17, 20

Pacific Islands 38
Pakistan 61
Paleolithic 31
Pearson, O. P. 49
Peru 40, 47, 84
Pharaoh 19
Phoenicians 41
photosynthesis 60, 69
pill 24
Ping-ti-Ho 32
pioneer 37
plague 31
plankton 30
Pleistocene 37, 38
polar ice-caps 60
Polish peasants 76
pollution 34, 35, 64–9, 89
poplar tree 72
population control 71–81
Portugal 38, 46
predators 27, 30
pressure, high blood 64
protozoa 20

Quechua Indians 47
quins 20

Ra 40, 41
rainfall 50, 51, 52, 53, 54
rat 20, 49, 64, 71
rat-flea 31
religion 24, 38

respiratory infections 34, 35, 44
Rome 27, 28, 75

Sahara 44, 45
Scotland 64
sexual intercourse 74, 75, 89
Siberia 37
skin disorders 64
snowshoe hare 10, 63, 64, 74
social influences 22, 46, 83, 89
South Africa 38
South America 16, 38, 43, 46, 85
Soviet Union 22, 42
spacecraft 55
Spain 38, 46
spermatozoa 21, 25
sterilization 77, 79

Stone Age 15, 17, 31, 49, 69
stress 17, 62–4, 69, 72
survivorship curves 28, 29
Sweden 24, 25

technology 38, 46, 49, 55, 86
territories 38, 49–51, 72, 74
thrips 71
Tierra del Fuego 38
tortoise 27
traditional peoples 17, 74, 75, 76, 78, 85, 89
transition theory 85, 86, 87, 89
tribe 49, 50, 52, 53, 54
Tristan da Cunha 46

ulcers 64

underdeveloped countries 28, 61, 71, 78, 83, 86
United States 11, 24, 38, 39, 42, 46, 49, 57, 77, 88, 89
urbanization 22

Vietnam 31

Wai Wai Indians 16
war 21, 32, 33, 35, 39, 89
water fleas 9
whale, blue 69
Wynne-Edwards, V. C. 72, 76, 78, 89

yeast cells 9, 17

Zambia 29

Acknowledgements

page
1   FAO Photo
2   Punch Publications Ltd
9   C. James Webb
11   Public Records Office
13   *Guardian*
16   Nicholas Guppy
18   *Sunday Express/Daily Mail/Sunday Express*
19   Radio Times Hulton Picture Library
21   Mary Evans Picture Library
23   Radio Times Hulton Picture Library/*Life* Magazine/Bill Leimbach
25   Associated Press Ltd
26   Camera Press Ltd
27, 31   British Museum/Mansell Collection
32   Novosti Press Agency
34–5   Gamma, Paris/Photo by Elliott Erwitt: Magnum Photos
36   *Sunday Times*
38   British Museum
39   Radio Times Hulton Picture Library
41   Keystone Press Agency Ltd
44–5   Photo by Gerster: Rapho
46   Paul Popper Ltd
48   Natural History Museum
50   Australian News & Information Bureau
54   Afrique Photo/Radio Times Hulton Picture Library
56   Camera Press Ltd
57   Mansell Collection
58–9   KLM Aerocarto
60   Paul Almasy
62–3   Drawing by Thelwell from *The Effluent Society* published by Methuen/Transworld Feature Syndicate
65–6   Camera Press Ltd
67   Syndication International/Rapho/Syndication International
68   Jean Suquet
69   Press Association Ltd
71   Punch Publications Ltd
73   Canadian Wild Life Service/Eric Hosking
75   Ron Cobb: Sawyer Press
76   Roger Viollet
77   Transworld Feature Syndicate
78–9   Photo by Mark Edwards/Camera Press Ltd
82   Rapho
83   Willy Ronis
84   Camera Press Ltd/*Empresa Editora*

Artists' credits

Penguin Education Illustration Department: 9, 10, 14, 15, 21, 22, 24, 27, 28, 30, 33, 37, 39, 40, 42, 43, 44, 46, 47, 51, 52, 53, 54, 55, 58, 64, 66, 72, 77, 80, 85, 86, 87, 88, 89.